EXPERIENCING THE

Holy SPIRIT

ANDREW MURRAY

EXPERIENCING THE

Holy SPIRIT

WHITAKER
HOUSE

Experiencing the Holy Spirit

ISBN: 979-8-88769-042-1
eBook ISBN: 978-1-60374-177-4
Printed in the United States of America
© 2024 by Whitaker House

Whitaker House
1030 Hunt Valley Circle
New Kensington, PA 15068
www.whitakerhouse.com

1 2 3 4 5 6 7 8 9 10 11 ᴜᴜ 30 29 28 27 26 25 24 23

CONTENTS

PREFACE

In all our studies of the work of the blessed Spirit, and in our pursuit of a life in His fullness, we will always find the sum of Christ's teaching in these wonderful words: *"He who believes in Me, as the Scripture has said, out of his heart will flow rivers of living water"* (John 7:38). As we are convicted of the defectiveness of our faith in Christ and as we understand that believing in Him means a yielding of the whole heart, life, and will, we can confidently count on receiving the Holy Spirit's power and presence. When Christ becomes all that God has made Him to be for us, the Holy Spirit can then flow from Christ to do His blessed work of leading us back to know Him better and to believe in Him more completely.

The book of Hebrews speaks of Christ in His heavenly glory and power as the object of our faith. The Holy Spirit reveals the way into the Holiest by the blood of Christ and invites us by faith in Christ to have our life there. As we yield our hearts to the leading of the Spirit to know Christ and to believe in what is revealed, the Spirit can take possession of us. The Spirit is given to reveal Christ, and every fully accepted revelation of Christ gives the Spirit room to dwell and work within us. This promise will surely then be fulfilled: *"He who believes in Me,...out of his heart will flow rivers of living water."* May God lead us to this simple and full faith in Christ, our great High Priest and King in the heavens, and so into a life in the fullness of the Spirit.

—Andrew Murray

INTRODUCTION

This book brings a simple but solemn message. The one thing needed for the church in its search for spiritual excellence is to be filled with the Spirit of God. In order to secure attention to this message and attract the hearts of my readers to its blessing, I have laid particular emphasis on certain main points:

+ The will of God for every one of His children is that they live entirely and unceasingly under the control of the Holy Spirit.

+ Without being filled with the Spirit, it is impossible for an individual Christian or a church to ever live or work as God desires.

+ In the life and experience of Christians, this blessing is little used and little searched for.

+ God waits to give us this blessing, and in our faith we may expect it with the greatest confidence.

+ The self-life and the world hinder and usurp the place that Christ ought to occupy.

+ We cannot be filled with the Spirit until we are prepared to yield ourselves to be led by the Lord Jesus—to forsake and sacrifice everything for this *"pearl of great price"* (Matt. 13:46).

We have such a poor idea of the unspiritual and sinful state that prevails in the church that, unless we take time to devote our hearts and our thoughts to the real facts of the case, the promise of God can make no deep impression on us. I have presented the subject in various aspects to prepare the way for the conviction that this blessing is in truth the one thing needed; and to get possession of this one thing, we ought to say goodbye to everything else we hold dear. Owing to the prevailing lack of the presence and operation of the Spirit, it takes a long time before these spiritual truths concerning the need, the fullness, and the reality of the Spirit's power can obtain mastery over us.

Every day ought to be a Pentecostal season in the church of Christ. Christians cannot live according to the will of God without this blessing. I cannot exhort you, my readers, strongly enough to continue this search for spiritual excellence by calling on God in the confidence that He will answer.

When we read the book of Acts, we see that the filling with the Spirit and His mighty operation was always obtained by prayer. Recall, for example, what took place at Antioch. When the Christians were engaged in fasting and prayer, God regarded them as prepared to receive the revelation that they must separate Barnabas and Saul. It was only after they had once more fasted and prayed that these two men went forth, sent by the Holy Spirit. (See Acts 13:2–3.) These servants of God felt that the blessing they needed could come only from above.

To obtain the blessing we so greatly need, we, in like manner, must liberate ourselves as far as possible from the demands of the earthly life. Let us never become weary or discouraged but ask that the Holy Spirit may again assume His rightful place and exercise full dominion in us. In addition, let us pray that He may again have His true place in the church, be held in honor by all, and in everything reveal the glory of our Lord Jesus. To the soul who diligently searches and prays in sincerity according to His Word, God's answer will surely come.

Nothing searches and cleanses the heart like true prayer. It teaches one to ask such questions as these: Do I really desire what I pray for? Am I willing to cast out everything to make room for what God is prepared to give me? Is the prayer of my lips really the prayer of my life? Am I willing to wait on Him, in quiet trust, until He gives me this supernatural gift—His own Spirit?

Let us pray continually, coming before God with supplications and strong crying as His priests and the representatives of His church. We can depend on Him to hear us.

Believer, you know that the Lord is a God who often hides Himself. He desires to be trusted. He is often very near to us without our knowing it. He is a God who knows His own time. Though He tarries, wait for Him. He will surely come. (See Habakkuk 2:3.)

1

HOW THE BLESSING IS TO BE TAUGHT

And it happened...that Paul...came to Ephesus. And finding some disciples he said to them, "Did you receive the Holy Spirit when you believed?"
—Acts 19:1–2

About twenty years after the outpouring of the Holy Spirit, this incident took place. In the course of his journey, Paul came to Ephesus and found in the Christian church some disciples in whom he observed that there was something lacking in their belief or experience. Accordingly he asked them the question, "Did you receive the Holy Spirit when you believed?" Their reply was that they had not even heard of the Holy Spirit. They had been baptized by disciples of John the Baptist with the baptism of repentance, with a view to faith in Jesus as One who was to come, but they were still unacquainted with the great event of the outpouring of the Spirit or the significance of it. They came from a region of the country into which the full Pentecostal preaching of the exalted Savior had not yet penetrated.

Paul took them at once under his care and told them about the full Gospel of the glorified Lord who had received the Spirit from the Father and had sent Him down to this world so that every one of His believing disciples might also receive Him. Hearing this good news and agreeing with it, they were baptized into the name of this Savior who baptizes with the Holy Spirit. Paul then laid his hands on them and prayed, and they received the Holy Spirit. They obtained a share in the Pentecostal miracle and spoke with other tongues.

In these chapters, it is my desire to bring to the children of God the message that there is a twofold Christian life. The one is that in which we experience something of the operations of the Holy Spirit, just as many did under the old covenant, but we do not yet receive Him as the Pentecostal Spirit, as the personal indwelling Guest. On the other hand, there is a more abundant life, in which the indwelling just referred to is known and experienced. When Christians come to fully understand the distinction between these two conditions, they will find the will of God concerning them.

Therefore, it is a possible experience for each believer, having confessed the sinfulness and inconsistency that still marks our lives, to dare to hope that the Christian community will once more be restored to its Pentecostal power. With our focus on this distinction, let's ponder the lessons presented in this incident at Ephesus.

DO NOT REST PREMATURELY

For a healthy Christian life, it is indispensable that we be fully conscious that we have received the Holy Spirit to dwell in us.

Had it been otherwise, Paul would never have asked the question, *"Did you receive the Holy Spirit when you believed?"* These disciples were recognized as believers. This position, however, was not enough for them. The disciples who walked with the Lord Jesus on earth were also true believers, yet He commanded them not to rest satisfied until they had received the Holy Spirit from Himself in heaven. Paul, too, had seen the Lord in His heavenly glory and was by that vision led to conversion. Yet even in his case, the spiritual work the Lord required to have done in him was not completed. Ananias had to go to him and lay his hands on him so that he might receive the Holy Spirit. Only then could he become a witness for Christ.

All these facts teach us that there are two ways in which the Holy Spirit works in us. The first is the preparatory operation in which He simply acts on us but does not yet take up His abode within us, though He leads us to conversion and faith and ever urges us to all that is good and holy. The second is the higher and more advanced phase of His working, when we receive Him as an abiding gift, as an indwelling Person who assumes responsibility for our whole inner beings. This is the ideal of the full Christian life.

WHERE DO WE STAND?

There are disciples of Christ who know little or nothing of this conscious indwelling of the Holy Spirit.

It is of the utmost importance to understand this statement. The more fully we come under the conviction of its truth, the better we will understand the condition of the church in our times and be enabled to discover where we really stand.

The condition I refer to becomes very plain to us when we consider what took place at Samaria. Philip the evangelist had preached there. Many had been led to believe in Jesus and were baptized into His name, and there was great joy in that city. When the apostles heard this news, they sent down Peter and John, who, when they came to Samaria, prayed that these new converts might receive the Holy Spirit. (See Acts 8:16–17.) This gift was something quite different from the working of the Spirit that led them to conversion, faith, and joy in Jesus as a Savior. It was something higher; for now from heaven and by the glorified Lord Himself, the Holy Spirit was imparted in power with His abiding indwelling to consecrate and fill their hearts.

If this new experience had not been given, the Samaritan disciples would still have been Christians, but they would have remained weak. Thus it is that in our own days, there are still many Christians who know nothing of this gift of the Holy Spirit. Amid much that is good and amiable, even with much earnestness and zeal, the lives of such Christians are still hampered by weakness, stumbling, and disappointment simply because they have never been brought into vitalizing contact with power from on high. Such souls have not received the Holy Spirit as the Pentecostal gift to be possessed, kept, and filled by Him.

CAN WE WORSHIP WITH SINCERITY?

It is the great work of the gospel ministry to lead believers to the Holy Spirit.

It was the great aim of the Lord Jesus, after He had educated and trained His disciples for three years, to lead them to the point of waiting for the promise of the Father and receiving the Holy Spirit sent down from heaven. This was the chief objective of Peter on the Day of Pentecost, when, after summoning those who were convicted in their hearts to repent and be baptized for the forgiveness of sins, he assured them that they should then receive the Holy Spirit. (See Acts 2:38.)

Paul aimed at this when he asked his fellow Christians if they did not know that they were each a temple of the Holy Spirit. He reminded them that they had to be filled with the Holy Spirit. (See Ephesians 5:18.)

Yes, the supreme need of the Christian life is to receive the Holy Spirit and, when we have it, to be conscious of the fact and live in harmony with it. An evangelical minister must not merely preach about the Holy Spirit from time to time, but also direct his efforts toward teaching his congregation that there can be no true worship except through the indwelling and unceasing operation of the Holy Spirit.

To lead believers to the Holy Spirit, the great lack in their lives must be pointed out to them.

This was the intention in Paul's question, *"Did you receive the Holy Spirit when you believed?"* Only those who are thirsty will drink water with eagerness, and only those who are sick will desire a physician. In the same way, it is only when believers are prepared to acknowledge the defective and sinful character of their spiritual condition that the preaching of the full blessing of Pentecost will find an entrance into their hearts.

Many Christians imagine that the only thing lacking in their lives is more earnestness or more strength and, if they only obtain these benefits, they will become all they ought to be. This makes the preaching of a full salvation of little avail. Only when the discovery is made that they are not standing in a right attitude toward the Holy Spirit, that they have only His preparatory operations but do not yet know Him in His indwelling, will the way to something higher ever be open or even be desired.

For this discovery, it is indispensable that the question should be put to each individual as pointedly and as personally as possible: *"Did you receive the Holy Spirit when you believed?"* When the answer takes the shape of a deeply felt and utterly sincere concern, then the time of revival is not far off.

HELP TO TAKE HOLD OF THIS BLESSING

In the Acts of the Apostles we read often about the laying on of hands and prayer. Even a man like Paul—whose conversion was due to the direct intervention of the Lord—had to receive the Spirit through laying on of hands and prayer on the part of Ananias. (See Acts 9:17.)

This implies that there must be among ministers of the Gospel, and believers in general, a power of the Spirit that makes them the channel of faith and courage to others. Those who are weak must be helped to take hold of the blessing for themselves. But those who have this blessing, as well as those who desire to have it, must realize and acknowledge their absolute dependence on the Lord and expect all from Him.

The gift of the Spirit is imparted only by God Himself. Every fresh outpouring of the Spirit comes from above. There must be frequent personal dealing with God. The minister of the Spirit whom God is to use for communicating the blessing, as well as the believer who is to receive it, must meet with God in immediate and close communion. *"Every good gift...is from above"* (James 1:17). Faith in this truth will give us courage to expect, with confidence and gladness, that the full Pentecostal blessing may be looked for and that a life under the continual leading of the Holy Spirit is within our reach.

The proclamation and the taking hold of this blessing will restore the Christian community to the primary Pentecostal power.

On the Day of Pentecost, speaking *"with other tongues"* (Acts 2:4) and prophesying were the results of being filled with the Spirit. Here at Ephesus, twenty years later, the very same miracle was again witnessed as the visible token and pledge of the other glorious gifts of the Spirit. We may depend on it that where the reception of the Holy Spirit and the possibility of being filled with Him are proclaimed and taken hold of, the blessed life of the Pentecostal community will be restored in all its fresh power.

An increasing acknowledgement of the lack of power in the church exists today. In spite of the multiplication of the means of grace, there is neither the power of the divine salvation in believers nor the power for conversion in preaching. Little conflict exists in the church between worldliness and unbelief.

This complaint is justified. If the expression of it became strong enough, the children of God might be led to cast themselves on the great truth that the Word of God teaches. When faith in the full Pentecostal blessing is found in the Christian church again, the members will find their strength and be able to do their first works.

THE CHURCH NEEDS MEN WHO TESTIFY

We need more pastors and teachers who preach Christ Jesus as John the Baptist did—as the One who baptizes with the Holy Spirit. It is only the minister who stands forth as a personal witness and living proof of the ministry of the Spirit whose word will have full entrance into the hearts of the people and exercise full sway over them. The first disciples obtained the baptism on their knees, and on their knees they obtained it for others. It will be on our knees also that the full blessing will be won today. Let this be the attitude in which we await the full blessing of our God.

Have you received the Holy Spirit since you believed? To be filled with the Holy Spirit of God and to have the full enjoyment of the Pentecostal blessing is the will of God concerning us. Judge your life and your work before the Lord in the light of this question, and present your answer to God.

Do not be afraid to confess before your Lord what is still lacking in you. Do not hold back, although you do not as yet fully understand what the blessing is or how it comes. The early disciples called on their Lord and waited with prayer and supplication.

Let your heart be filled with a deep conviction of what you lack, a desire for what God offers, and a willingness to sacrifice everything for it. Then you may rest assured that the marvel of Jerusalem and Samaria, of Caesarea and Ephesus, will once again be repeated. We may and we will be filled with the Spirit.

2

HOW GLORIOUS THE
BLESSING IS

They were all filled with the Holy Spirit.
—Acts 2:4

Whenever we speak of being filled with the Holy Spirit and desire to know precisely what it is, our thoughts always turn back to the Day of Pentecost. How glorious the blessing is that is brought from heaven by the Holy Spirit!

One fact makes the great event of the Day of Pentecost doubly instructive—namely, that, by their three-year relationship with the Lord Jesus, we have learned to know intimately the men who were then filled with the Spirit. Their weaknesses, defects, sins, and perversities all stand open to our view.

The blessing of Pentecost brought about a complete transformation. They became entirely new men, so that one could say of them with truth, *"Old things have passed away; behold, all things have become new"* (2 Cor. 5:17). Close study of them and their example will help us in more than one way. It shows us to what weak and sinful men the Spirit will come. It teaches us how they were prepared for the blessing. It teaches us also—and this is the principal thing—how mighty and complete the transformation is when the Holy Spirit is received in His fullness. It lets us see how glorious is the grace that awaits us if we diligently search for spiritual excellence through the full blessing of Pentecost.

BLESSINGS OF THE PENTECOSTAL LIFE

The ever-abiding presence and indwelling of the Lord Jesus is the first and principal blessing of the Pentecostal life. In the course of our Lord's dealings with His disciples on earth, He spared no pains to teach and train them or to renew and sanctify them. In most respects, however, they remained just what they were. The reason was that, up to this point, He was still nothing more than an external Christ who stood outside of them and from the outside sought to work on them by His word and His personal influence.

With the advent of Pentecost, this condition was entirely changed. In the Holy Spirit, He came down as the indwelling Christ to become the life of their lives. He had promised this in the words, *"I will not leave you orphans; I will come to you....At that day you will know that I am in My Father, and you in Me, and I in you"* (John 14:18, 20).

This was the source of all the other blessings that came with Pentecost. Jesus Christ, the Crucified, came in spiritual power to impart to them the ever-abiding presence of their Lord in a way that was intimate and all-powerful. Him whom they had had in the flesh, living with them on earth, they now received by the Spirit in His heavenly glory within them. Instead of an outward Jesus near them, they now obtained the inward Jesus with them.

From this first and principal blessing sprang the second: the Spirit of Jesus came into them as the life and the power of sanctification. Often the Lord had to rebuke the disciples for their pride and exhort them to humility. It was all of no avail. Even on the last night of His earthly life, at the table of the Holy Supper, there was strife among them as to which of them should be the greatest. (See Luke 22:24.)

The outward teaching of the outward Christ, whatever other influences it may have exercised, was not sufficient to redeem them from the power of indwelling sin. This could be achieved only by the indwelling Christ. Only when Jesus descended into them by the Holy Spirit did they undergo a complete change. They received Him in His heavenly humility and subjection to the Father and in His self-sacrifice for others. From that point, all was changed. From that moment on, they were animated by the spirit of the meek and lowly Jesus.

Many Christians keep their minds occupied only with the external Christ on the cross. They wait for the blessing of His teaching and His working without understanding that the blessing of Pentecost brings Him *into us*. This is why they make so little progress in sanctification. Christ Himself is our sanctification (1 Cor. 1:30).

LIVING THE LIFE OF LOVE

A heart overflowing with the love of God is also a part of the blessing of Pentecost. Next to pride, a lack of love was the sin for which the Lord had often rebuked His disciples. These two sins have the same root: the desire for pleasing self. The new commandment that He gave them, by which all men would know that they were His disciples, was their love for one another.

This was gloriously manifested on the Day of Pentecost when the Spirit of the Lord poured out His love in the hearts of His own. (See Romans 5:5.) *"The multitude of those who believed were of one heart and one soul"* (Acts 4:32). All things they possessed were held in common. No one said that anything he had was his own. The kingdom of heaven, with its life of love, had come down to them. The spirit, the disposition, and the wonderful love of Jesus filled them because He Himself had come into them.

The mighty working of the Spirit and the indwelling of the Lord Jesus are bound together with a life of love. This appears in the prayer of Paul on behalf of the Ephesians. He asked that they might be strengthened with power by the Spirit in order that Christ might dwell in their hearts (Eph. 3:17). Then he quickly made this addition: *"That you, being rooted and grounded in love, may be able to comprehend with all the saints…the love… which passes knowledge"* (vv. 17–19).

The filling with the Spirit and the indwelling of Christ bring a life that has its root, its joy, its power, and its evidence in love because Christ is love. If the filling with the Spirit was recognized as the blessing that the Father promised us, the love of God would fill the church, and the world would be convinced she has received a heavenly element into her life.

OBTAINING COURAGE AND POWER

We know how Peter denied his Lord and how all the disciples fled and forsook Him. Their hearts were really attached to the Lord, and they were sincerely willing to do what they had promised and go to die with Him. But when it came to the crisis, they had neither the courage nor the power. After the blessing of the Spirit of Pentecost, it was no longer a matter of willing apart from performing. By Christ dwelling in us, God works both the willing and the doing (Phil. 2:13).

On the Day of Pentecost, Peter preached about Jesus to thousands of hostile Jews. With boldness and in opposition to the leaders of the people, he was able to say, *"We ought to obey God rather than men"* (Acts 5:29). With courage and joy, Stephen, Paul, and many others were enabled to encounter threats, suffering, and death. They did this triumphantly because the Spirit of Christ—the Victor, Christ Himself—had been glorified and now dwelt within them. The joy of the blessing of Pentecost gives courage and power to speak for Jesus because it fills the whole heart with Him.

The blessing of Pentecost makes the Word of God new. We see this fact distinctly in the case of the disciples. As with all the Jews of that age, their ideas of the Messiah and the kingdom of

God were external and carnal. All the instruction of the Lord Jesus throughout three long years could not change their way of thinking. They were unable to comprehend the doctrine of a suffering and dying Messiah or the hope of His invisible spiritual dominion. Even after His resurrection, He had to rebuke them for their unbelieving spirit and their inability to understand the Scriptures.

With the coming of the Day of Pentecost, an entire change took place. Their ancient Scriptures opened up before them. The light of the Holy Spirit in them illuminated the Word. In the preaching of Peter and Stephen and in the addresses of Paul and James, we see how a divine light had shone on the Old Testament. They saw everything through the Spirit of this Jesus who had made His abode within them.

So it will be with us. It is necessary to meditate on the Scriptures and keep the Word of God in our thoughts, hearts, and daily walks. Let us, however, constantly remember that only when we are filled with the Spirit can we fully experience the spiritual power and truth of the Word. He is *"the Spirit of truth"* (John 16:13). He alone guides us into all truth when He dwells in us.

POWER TO BLESS OTHERS

The divine power of the exalted Jesus to grant repentance and the forgiveness of sins is exercised by Him through His servants. The minister of the Gospel who desires to preach repentance and forgiveness through Jesus and have success in winning souls must do the work in the power of the Spirit of Jesus. Much preaching of conversion and pardon is fruitless because these elements of truth are presented only as a doctrine.

Some preachers try to reach the hearts of their audience in the power of mere human earnestness, reasoning, and eloquence. But little blessing is won by these means. The man whose chief desire is to be filled with the Spirit of the indwelling Christ can be assured that the glorified Lord will speak and work in him. He will obtain the blessing—not always in the same manner, but it will always certainly come.

In preaching and in the daily life of a servant of Christ, the full blessing of Pentecost is the sure way of becoming a blessing to others. Jesus said, *"He who believes in Me,...out of his heart will flow rivers of living water"* (John 7:38). This refers to the Holy Spirit. A heart filled with the Spirit will overflow with the Spirit.

It is the blessing of Pentecost that will make the church what God wants her to be.

I have spoken of what the Spirit will do in individual believers. Think of what the blessing will be when the church as a whole answers her calling to be filled with the Spirit and exhibits the life, the power, and the very presence of her Lord to the world. We must not only seek and receive this blessing, each person for himself, but we must also remember that the full manifestation of the blessing cannot be given until the whole body of Christ receives it. *"If one member suffers, all the members suffer with it"* (1 Cor. 12:26).

If many members of the church of Christ are content to remain without this blessing, the whole church will suffer. Even in individual disciples, the blessing will not come to its full manifestation. Therefore, it is of the utmost importance that we not only think of what being filled with the Spirit means for ourselves, but also consider what it will do for the church.

WILL YOU SEPARATE YOURSELF?

Recall the morning of the Day of Pentecost. At that time, the Christian church in Jerusalem consisted only of one hundred and twenty disciples, most of them poor, uneducated fishermen, tax collectors, and humble women, an insignificant and despised gathering. Yet it was by these believers that the kingdom of God had to be proclaimed and extended, and they did it.

By them and those who were added to them, the power of Jewish prejudice and of pagan hardness of heart was overcome, and the church of Christ won glorious triumphs. This grand result was achieved simply and only because the first Christian church was filled with the Spirit. The members of it gave themselves wholly to their Lord. They allowed themselves to be filled, consecrated, governed, and used only by Him. They yielded themselves to Him as instruments of His power. He dwelt in them and used them for all His wondrous deeds.

It is to this same experience that the church of Christ in our age must be brought back. This is the only thing that will help her in the conflict with sin and the world. She must be filled with the Spirit.

Beloved fellow Christians, this call comes to you and the whole church of the Lord. This one thing is needed: we have to be filled with the Spirit. Do not imagine that you must understand it all before you seek and find it. For those who wait on Him, God will do more than they can imagine. You must taste the happiness and know by personal experience the blessedness of having Jesus in your heart. Then His Spirit of holiness and humility, of love and self-sacrifice, and of courage and power will become as natural as your own spirit.

If you have the Word of God in you, you will be able to carry it as a blessing to others. If you desire to see the church of Christ arrayed in her first splendor, then separate yourselves from everything that is evil, cast it out of your hearts, and focus your desire on this one thing: to be filled with the Spirit of God. Receive this blessing as your rightful heritage. Take hold of it and hold on to it by faith. It will certainly be given to you.

HOW THE BLESSING WAS BESTOWED FROM HEAVEN

If you love Me, keep My commandments. And I will pray the Father, and He will give you another Helper, that He may abide with you forever; the Spirit of truth.
—John 14:15–17

A tree always lives according to the nature of the seed from which it grew. Every living being is always guided and governed by the nature that it received at its birth. The church received the promise and her growth by the Holy Spirit on the day of her birth. It is important for us to turn back often to the Day of Pentecost and not to rest until we thoroughly understand, receive, and experience what God did for His people on that Day. The hearts of the disciples were ready to receive the Spirit. Now we know what we must do to enjoy the same blessing. The first disciples serve as our examples on the way to the fullness of the Spirit.

What enabled them to become the recipients of these heavenly gifts? What made them acceptable vessels for the habitation of God? The right answer to these questions will help us on the way to being filled with the Holy Spirit.

A PERSONAL RELATIONSHIP

First, the disciples were deeply attached to the Lord Jesus. The Son of God came into the world in order to unite the divine life, which He had with the Father, with the life of man. In this way, the life of God could penetrate the life of the creature. When He had completed the work by His obedience, death, and resurrection, He was exalted to the throne of God on high. This was done in order that, in spiritual power, His disciples and church might participate in His very own life. We read that the Holy Spirit *"was not yet given, because Jesus was not yet glorified"* (John 7:39). It was only after His glorification that the Spirit of the complete indwelling of God in man could be given. It is the Spirit of the glorified Jesus that the disciples received on the Day of Pentecost. His Spirit penetrated all the members of His body.

If the fullness of the Spirit dwells in Jesus, a personal relationship with Him is the first condition for the reception of the full gift of the Comforter. It was to attain this end that the Lord Jesus kept the disciples in close fellowship with Himself. He desired to attach them to Himself. He wanted them to truly feel at one with Him. He wanted them to identify themselves with Him, as far as this was possible. By knowledge, love, and obedience, they became inwardly knit to Him. This was the preparation for participating in the Spirit of His glorification.

The lesson that is taught here is extremely simple, but it is one of profound significance. Many Christians believe in the Lord, are zealous in His service, and eagerly desire to become holy, yet they do not succeed in their endeavor. It often seems as if they could not understand the promise of the Spirit. The thought of being filled with the Spirit exercises little influence on them.

The reason is obvious. They lack the personal relationship to the Lord Jesus, the inward attachment to Him, the perfectly natural reference to Him as their best and nearest Friend, as the beloved Lord, that was so characteristic of the disciples. This is absolutely indispensable. Only a heart that is entirely occupied with the Lord Jesus and depends entirely on Him can hope for the fullness of the Spirit.

THEY LEFT ALL FOR JESUS

"Nothing for nothing." This proverb contains a deep truth. A thing that costs me nothing may nevertheless cost me much. It may bring me under an obligation to the giver and so cost me more than it is worth. I may have so much trouble in taking hold of it and keeping it that I may pay much more for it than the price that should be asked for it. "Nothing for nothing."

This maxim also holds good in the life of the kingdom of heaven. The parables of the *"treasure hidden in a field"* (Matt. 13:44) and the *"pearl of great price"* (v. 46) teach us that, in order to obtain possession of the kingdom within us, we must sell all that we have. This is the renunciation that Jesus literally demanded of the disciples who followed Him. This is the requirement He so often repeated in His preaching: *"Whoever of you does not forsake all that he has cannot be My disciple"* (Luke 14:33).

The two worlds between which we stand are in direct conflict with one another. The world we live in exercises such a mighty influence over us that it is often necessary for us to withdraw from it. Jesus trained His disciples to long for what is heavenly. Only then could He prepare them to desire and receive the heavenly gift with an undivided heart.

The Lord has left us no outward directions as to how much of the world we are to abandon or in what manner we are to do so. In His Word He teaches us that without sacrifice, without a deliberate separation from the world, we will never make much progress in grace. The spirit of this world has penetrated into us so deeply that we do not observe it. We share in its desire for comfort and enjoyment, for self-pleasing and self-exaltation, without our knowing how impossible these things make it for us to be filled with the Spirit.

Let us learn from the early disciples that, to be filled from the heavenly world with the Spirit, we must be entirely separate from the children of this world or from worldly Christians. We must be willing to live as entirely different people, who literally represent heaven on earth, because we have received the Spirit of the King of heaven.

RECOGNIZING YOUR ENEMIES

Man has two great enemies by whom the Devil tempts him and with whom he has to contend. The one is the world outside, and the other is the self-life within. This last, the selfish ego, is much more dangerous and stronger than the first. It is quite possible for a man to have made much progress in forsaking the world while the self-life retains full dominion within him.

You see this fact illustrated in the case of the disciples. Peter could say with truth, *"See, we have left all and followed You"* (Matt. 19:27). Yet how manifestly did the selfish ego, with its self-pleasing and its self-confidence, still retain its full sway over him.

The Lord led the disciples to the point of forsaking their outward possessions and following Him. He also began to teach them that a disciple must deny himself and lose his own life if he wishes to be worthy of receiving His life. It was man's love for his self-life that hindered the Lord Jesus from doing His work in man's heart. It cost man more to be redeemed from the selfish ego within him than to withdraw from the world around him. The self-life is the natural life of sinful man. He can be liberated from it by nothing except death—that is, by first dying to it and then living in the strength of the new life that comes from God.

The forsaking of the world began at the outset of the three years' discipleship. At the end of that period, at the Cross of Jesus, dying to the self-life first took place. When they saw Him die, they learned to despair of themselves and of everything on which they had previously based their hope. Whether they had thought of their Lord and the expected redemption or of themselves and their shameful unfaithfulness toward Him, they tended to be filled with despair over everything. Little did they know that this despair would break up their hard hearts, mortifying their self-life and confidence in themselves. This death to self enabled them to receive something entirely new—namely, a divine life through the Spirit of the glorified Jesus in the innermost depths of their souls.

Oh, that we understood better that nothing hampers us as much as secret reliance on ourselves. On the other hand, nothing brings as much blessing as entire despair of ourselves and all that is on the earth, teaching us to turn our hearts wholly to heaven and partake of the heavenly gift.

THE UNHEARD-OF WONDER

The disciples received and held fast the promise of the Spirit given by the Lord Jesus.

In His farewell address, Jesus comforted His disciples in their sorrow over His departure with one great promise— namely, the mission of the Holy Spirit from heaven. Better than His bodily presence among them, it would be to them the full fruit and the power of His redemption. The divine life—He Himself with the Father—was to make its abode within them. They were to know they were in Him and He in them. At His ascension from the Mount of Olives, this promise of the Spirit was the last subject He addressed to them.

It is evident the disciples had little idea of what this promise signified. But however defective their understanding was, they held it fast; or rather, the promise held them fast and would not let them go. They all had only one thought: "Something has been promised to us by our Lord; it will give us a share in

His heavenly power and glory; we know for certain that it is coming." What the thing itself was or what their experience of it was to be, they could give no account. It was enough for them that they had the word of the Lord. He would make it a blessed reality within them.

The same disposition is needed now. To us also, even as to them, has the word of the Lord come concerning the Spirit who is to descend from the throne in the power of His glorified life.

"He who believes in Me,...out of his heart will flow rivers of living water" (John 7:38). For us also the one thing needed is to hold fast to that word, to set our whole desire on the fulfillment of it, and to lay aside all else until we inherit the promise. The word from the mouth of Jesus, concerning the reception of the Spirit in such measure that we will be endued with power from on high, must fill us with strong desire and with firm, joyful assurance.

They waited on the Father until the fulfillment of the promise came and they were filled with the Spirit.

The ten days of waiting were for them days in which they were continually praising and blessing God and continuing in prayer and supplication. It is not enough for us to try to strengthen desire and to hold fast our confidence. The principal thing is to set ourselves in close and abiding contact with God. The blessing must come from God; God Himself must give it to us. We are to receive the gift directly from Him. What is promised to us is a wonderful work of divine omnipotence and love. What we desire is the personal occupancy and indwelling of God the Holy Spirit. God Himself must give this personally to us.

A man gives another a piece of bread or a piece of money. He gives it away and has nothing further to do with it. It is not so with God's gift of the Holy Spirit. No, the Spirit is God. God is in the Spirit who comes to us, even as He was in the Son. The gift of the Spirit is the most personal act of the Godhead. It is the gift of Himself to us. We have to receive it in the closest, personal contact with God.

The clearer the insight we obtain into this principle, the more deeply we will feel how little we can do to grasp the blessing by our own desiring or believing. The goodness of God alone must give it. His omnipotence must work it into us. Our disposition must be one of silent assurance that the Father desires to give it to us and will not keep us waiting one moment longer than is absolutely necessary. Every soul that persists in waiting will be filled with the glory of God.

Every tree grows from the root out of which it first sprang. The Day of Pentecost was the planting of the Christian church, and the Holy Spirit became the power of its life. Let us turn back to that experience and learn from the disciples what is really necessary. Attachment to Jesus, the abandonment of everything in the world for Him, despair of self and of all help from man, holding on to the word of promise, and then waiting on the living God—this is the sure way of living in the joy and power of the Holy Spirit.

4

HOW LITTLE THE BLESSING IS ENJOYED

My speech and my preaching were not with persuasive
words of human wisdom, but in demonstration of the
Spirit and of power, that your faith should not be in the
wisdom of men but in the power of God.
—1 Corinthians 2:4–5

Paul spoke here of two kinds of preaching and two kinds of faith. The spirit of the preacher will determine the faith of the congregation. When the preaching of the Cross is given only in the words of human wisdom, then the faith of the hearers will be in the wisdom of men. When the preaching is in demonstration of the Spirit and of power, the faith of the Christian people will also be firm and strong in the power of God. Preaching in the demonstration of the Spirit will bring the double blessing of power in the Word and in the faith of those who receive that Word. If we desire to know the measure of the working of the Spirit, we must consider the preaching and the faith that spring from it. In this way alone can we see whether the full blessing of Pentecost is truly manifested in the church.

Very few individuals are prepared to say this is really the case. Everywhere among the children of God, we hear complaints of weakness and sin. Among those who do not complain is reason to fear that their silence is ascribed to ignorance or self-satisfaction. It is important that we concentrate on this fact until we come under the full conviction that the condition of the church is marked by powerlessness and that nothing can restore her except the return to a life in the full enjoyment of the blessing of Pentecost. The more deeply we feel our deficiency, the more speedily we will desire and obtain restoration. It will help to awaken longing for this blessing if we earnestly consider how little it is enjoyed in the church and how far the church is from being what her Lord has power to make her.

POWER OVER SIN

Think, for example, what little power over sin there is among the children of God.

The Spirit of Pentecost is the Holy Spirit, the Spirit of God's holiness. When He filled the hearts of the disciples, a transformation was brought about in them. Their carnal thoughts were changed into spiritual insight, their pride into humility, their selfishness into love, their fear of man into courage and fidelity. Sin was cast out by the inflowing of the life of Jesus and of heaven.

The life that the Lord has prepared for His people is a life of victory. It is not victory to such an extent that there will be no temptation to evil or inclination to sin. But there is to be victory of such a kind that the indwelling power of the Spirit who fills us, the presence of the indwelling Savior, will keep sin in subjection as the light subdues the darkness.

Yet to what a small extent we see power for victory over sin in the church! Even among earnest Christians we see untruthfulness and lack of honor, pride and self-esteem, selfishness and lack of love. How little are the traces of the image of Jesus—obedience, humility, love, and entire surrender to the will of God—even among the people of God! The truth is that we have become so accustomed to the confession of sin and unfaithfulness, of disobedience and backsliding, that it is no longer regarded as a matter of shame.

We make the confession before each other; and then after the prayer, we rest comforted and contented. Brothers and sisters, let us feel humbled and mourn over it! It is because so little of the full blessing of the Spirit is enjoyed or sought that the children of God still commit so much sin and have so much to confess.

Let every sin, whether in ourselves or others, serve as a call to notice how much the Spirit of God is lacking among us. Let every instance of failure, in the fear of the Lord, in love, holiness, and entire surrender to the will of God, urge us to call on God to bring His Spirit to full dominion over the church once more.

SEPARATION FROM THE WORLD

When the Lord Jesus promised the Comforter, He said, *"Whom the world cannot receive"* (John 14:17). The spirit of this world, which is devotion to the visible, is in irreconcilable antagonism with the Spirit of Jesus in heaven, where God and His will are everything. The world has rejected the Lord Jesus; and, to whatever extent it may now usurp the Christian name, the world is still the same untamable enemy.

For this reason Jesus said of His disciples, *"They are not of the world, just as I am not of the world"* (John 17:16). This, too, is the reason why Paul said, *"We have received, not the spirit of the world, but the Spirit who is from God"* (1 Cor. 2:12). The two spirits, the spirit of the world and the Spirit of God, are engaged in a life-and-death conflict with one another.

This is why God has always called on His people to separate themselves from the world and to live as pilgrims whose treasure and hearts are in heaven. But is this what is really seen among Christians? Who will dare to say so? When they have attained a measure of unblamableness in their walk and assurance of heaven, most Christians consider that they are at liberty to enjoy the world as fully as others. Little is seen of true heavenly mindedness in conversation and walk or in disposition and endeavor. Is this not the case because the search for spiritual excellence is so little enjoyed and sought?

Light drives out darkness. The Spirit of heaven expels the spirit of the world. Where a man does not surrender himself to be filled with the Spirit of Jesus and the Spirit of heaven, though he may be very Christian, he must come under the power of the spirit of the world. Listen to the piercing cry that rises from the whole church, "Who will rescue us from the power of this spirit of the world?" Your answer should be, "Nothing, no one, except the Spirit of God. You must be filled with the Spirit."

ARE WE STEADFAST?

Those who labor for the salvation of souls complain that there are many who are full of zeal for a time and then fall away. When professing Christians enter into another circle of influence and are put to the test of prosperity or temptation, they cease to persevere. What produces this unfortunate result? It comes from preaching with the wisdom of persuasive words rather than in demonstration of the Spirit and of power. Hence their faith also stands in the wisdom and work of man rather than in the power of God.

As long as such people have the benefit of earnest and instructive preaching, they will continue to stand. If they lose it, they will begin to backslide. Because current preaching shows little demonstration of the Spirit, souls are not brought into contact with the living God. For the same reason, far too much of the current faith is not in the power of God.

The Word, preaching, and means of grace will become a hindrance instead of a help if they are not in demonstration of the Spirit. All external means of grace are things that inevitably change and fade. The Spirit alone works a faith that stands in the power of God and so remains strong and unwavering.

Why are there so many who do not continue to stand? The answer of God is a grave lack of the demonstration of the Spirit. Let every sad example serve as a summons to us to acknowledge that the full blessing of Pentecost is lost. This is what we long for and must have from God. Let all that is within us begin to thirst and cry out, "Come from the four winds, Spirit of God, and breathe on these dead souls so that they may live." Think how little there is of power for service among the unconverted.

What an immense host of workers there is in Christian countries. How varied and unceasing is the preaching of the Word. Sunday school teachers are numbered by hundreds of thousands. Large numbers of Christian parents make their children acquainted with the Word of God and also bring them to the Lord as Savior. Yet how little fruit springs from all this work.

Many who hear and are by no means indifferent never make a definite choice for salvation. Many who from youth to old age are familiar with the Word of God are never seized by it in the depths of their hearts. They find it good, pleasing, and instructive to attend church, but they have never felt the power of the Word as a hammer, a sword, or a fire. The reason they are so little disturbed is that the preaching they listen to is so little in demonstration of the Spirit and of power. This is evidence enough that there is a great lack of the full blessing of Pentecost.

Does the blame for this issue belong to preachers or to congregations? I feel it belongs to both. Preachers are the offspring of the Christian community. Through children we are enabled to see whether parents are spiritually healthy or not. Likewise, preachers are dependent on the life that is in their congregations.

When a congregation finds satisfaction in the merely acceptable and instructive preaching of a young minister, it encourages him to go forward on the same path. He should rather be helped by its more advanced believers to seek earnestly the demonstration of the Spirit. When a minister does not lead his congregation to expect everything from the Spirit of God, then he is tempted to put confidence in the wisdom of man and the work of man.

The great cause of all worldliness and impenitence is the lack of the full blessing of Pentecost. This alone gives power from on high that can break down and revive the hard hearts of men.

A SOURCE OF COURAGE

Think how little preparedness there is for self-sacrifice on behalf of the extension of the kingdom of God.

When the Lord Jesus promised the Holy Spirit at His ascension, it was given as a power in us to work for Him. *"You shall receive power when the Holy Spirit has come upon you; and you shall be witnesses to Me in Jerusalem, and in all Judea and Samaria, and to the end of the earth"* (Acts 1:8). The aim of the Pentecostal blessing from the King in heaven was simply to complete the equipping of His servants for His work as King on the earth. No sooner did the Spirit descend on them than they began to witness for Him. The Spirit filled them with the desire, impulse, courage, and power to brave all hostility and danger and to endure all suffering and persecution in making Jesus known as a Savior. The Spirit of Pentecost was the true missionary spirit that seeks to win the whole world for Jesus Christ.

It is often said in our days that the missionary spirit is on the increase. Yet when we reflect carefully how little effort is expended on the missionary enterprise in comparison with the time spent on our own interests, we will see at once how feebly this question is still kindled in our hearts: "What more can I still sacrifice for Jesus? He offered Himself for me. I will offer myself wholly for Him and His work."

It has been well said that the Lord measures our gifts not according to what we give, but according to what we retain. He who stands beside the treasury and observes what is cast into it still finds many who, like the widow, cast in their entire living. (See Mark 12:41–44.)

So many people have given only what they could never miss and what costs them little or no sacrifice. How different it would be if the full blessing of Pentecost began to flow in. How the hearts of men would burn with love for Jesus and, out of sheer joy, be impelled to give everything so that He might be known as Savior and so that all might know His love.

Brother or sister, contemplate the condition of the church on earth, of the Christian community around you, and of your own heart. Then see why there is grave reason for the cry, "The full blessing of Pentecost—how little it is known!" Ponder the present lack of sanctification, of separation from the world, of steadfastness among professing Christians, of conversions among the unsaved, and of self-sacrifice for the kingdom of God. Let the sad reality deepen in your soul the conviction that the church is at present suffering from one great evil, and this is her lack of the blessing of Pentecost. There can be no healing of her breaches, no restoration from her fall, and no renewing of her power except by this one remedy—namely, her being filled with the Spirit of God.

Never cease to speak, think, mourn, and pray over this trouble until this one necessary thing becomes the one thing that occupies our hearts. Restoration is not easy. It may not come all at once. It may not come quickly. The disciples of Jesus required every day with Jesus for three long years to prepare them for it.

Let us not be unduly discouraged if the transformation we long for does not take place immediately. Let us feel the need and take it to heart. Let us continue to be steadfast in prayer. Let us stand fast in faith.

The blessing of Pentecost is the birthright of the church, the pledge of our inheritance, and something that belongs to us here on earth. Faith can never be put to shame. Cleaving to Jesus with purpose of heart can never be in vain. The hour will surely come when, if we believe perseveringly in Him, out of our hearts *will flow rivers of living water* (John 7:38).

5

HOW THE BLESSING
IS HINDERED

*Then Jesus said to His disciples, "If anyone desires to come
after Me, let him deny himself, and take up his cross, and
follow Me. For whoever desires to save his life will lose it,
but whoever loses his life for My sake will find it."*
—Matthew 16:24–25

M any people earnestly seek the full blessing of Pentecost
and yet do not find it. Often the question is asked as to what
may be the cause of this failure. To this inquiry more than one

answer may be given. Sometimes the solution to the problem points in the direction of one or another sin that is still permitted. Worldliness, lovelessness, lack of humility, and ignorance of the secret of walking in the way of faith, and indeed many more causes, may also be often mentioned in truth.

Many people think they have come to the Lord and sincerely confessed these failures and put them away. Yet they complain that the blessing does not come. It is necessary to point out that there still remains one great hindrance—namely, the root from which all other hindrances have their beginning. This root is nothing less than the individual self, the hidden life of *self* with its varied forms of self-seeking, self-pleasing, self-confidence, and self-satisfaction.

The more earnestly anyone strives to obtain the blessing and desires to know what prevents him, the more certainly he will be led to the discovery that it is here the great evil lies. He himself is his worst enemy. He must be liberated from himself, and the self-life to which he clings must be utterly lost. Only then can the life of God entirely fill him.

A FULL UNDERSTANDING OF THE CROSS

This is what is taught in the words of the Lord Jesus to Peter. Peter had uttered such a glorious confession of his Lord that Jesus said to him, *"Blessed are you, Simon Bar-Jonah, for flesh and blood has not revealed this to you, but My Father who is in heaven"* (Matt. 16:17). But when the Lord began to speak of His death by crucifixion, the same Peter was seduced by Satan to say, *"Far be it from You, Lord; this shall not happen to You!"* (v. 22).

The Lord said to him that not only must He Himself lay down His life, but also this same sacrifice was to be made by every disciple. Every disciple must deny himself and take up his cross in order that he himself may be crucified and put to death on it. He who wishes to save his life will lose it, and he who is prepared to lose his life for Christ's sake will find it.

You see, then, what the Lord teaches and requires. Peter had learned through the Father to know Christ as the Son of God, but he did not yet know Him as the Crucified One. Of the absolute necessity of the death on the cross, he as yet knew nothing. It may be so with the Christian. He knows the Lord Jesus as his Savior; he desires to know Him better, but he does not yet understand that he must have a deeper discernment of the death of the cross as a death which he himself must die. He must actually deny and lose his life—his whole life and being in the world—before he can receive the full life of God.

This requirement is hard and difficult. And why is this so? Why should a Christian be called on always to deny himself, his own feelings, will, and pleasure? Why must he part with his life? The answer is very simple. It is because that life is so completely under the power of sin and death that it has to be utterly denied and sacrificed. The self-life must be wholly taken away to make room for the life of God. He who wishes to have the full, overflowing life of God must utterly deny and lose his own life.

Only one great stumbling block lies in the way of the full blessing of Pentecost. It is the fact that two opposing things cannot at the same time occupy the very same place. Your own life and the life of God cannot fill the heart at the same time. Your life hinders the entrance of the life of God. When your own life is cast out, the life of God will fill you. As long as I myself am still something, Jesus Himself cannot be everything. My life must be expelled; then the Spirit of Jesus will flow in.

Let every seeker of the full blessing of Pentecost accept this principle and hold on to it. The subject is of such importance that I would like to make it still clearer by pointing out the chief lessons that these words of the Lord Jesus teach us.

SELF AND THE POWER OF SIN

When God created the angels and man, He gave them a separate personality, a power over themselves, with the intention that they would, of their own free will, present and offer up that life to Him in order that He in turn might fill them with His life and His glory. To be a vessel filled with the life and the perfection of God was to be the highest blessedness of the creature.

The fall of angels and men alike consisted of nothing but the perversion of their lives, their wills, and their personalities, away from God, in order to please themselves. This self-exaltation was the pride that cast them out of heaven and into hell. This pride was the infernal poison that the Serpent breathed into the ears and the heart of Eve.

Man turned himself away from God to delight in himself and the world. His life, his whole individuality, was perverted and withdrawn from the control of God so that he might seek and serve himself.

You must utterly lose that life before the full life of the Spirit of God can be yours. To the minutest details, always and in everything, you must deny that self-life! *"If anyone desires to come after Me, let him deny himself, and take up his cross, and follow Me."*

A deep conviction of the entire corruption of our human nature is an experience that is still lacking in many people. It appears to them both strange and harsh when we say that in nothing is the Christian free to follow his own feelings. Self-denial is a requirement that must prevail in every sphere of life and without any exceptions. The Lord has never withdrawn His words: *"Whoever of you does not forsake all that he has cannot be My disciple"* (Luke 14:33).

IS YOUR HEART OPEN?

At the time of his conversion, the young Christian has little understanding of this requirement. He receives the seed of the new life into his heart while the natural life is still strong. It was this way with Peter when the Lord addressed to him the above words. He was a disciple but an incomplete one. When his Lord was to die, instead of denying himself, he denied his Lord. But this grievous failure brought him at last to despair of himself and prepared him for losing his own life entirely and for being wholly filled with the life of Jesus.

We must all eventually come to this point. As long as a Christian imagines that in some things—for example, in his eating and drinking, in the spending of his time or money, or in his thinking and speaking about others—he has the right and the liberty to follow his own wishes, to please himself, and to maintain his own life, he cannot possibly attain the full blessing of Pentecost.

My dear readers, it is an unspeakably holy and glorious thing that a man can be filled with the Spirit of God. It demands inevitably that the present occupant and governor of the heart, the individual self, be cast out and everything be surrendered into the hands of the new inhabitant, the Spirit of God. If only we could understand that the joy and power of being filled with the Spirit will come once we comply with the first and principal condition—namely, that He alone be acknowledged as our Life and our Leader.

WHO PERFORMS THIS TRANSFORMATION?

At no stage of our spiritual careers are the power and the deceitfulness of the individual self and the self-life more manifest than in the attempt to grasp the full blessing of Pentecost. Many people endeavor to take hold of this blessing by a great variety of efforts. They do not succeed and are not able to discover the reason why. They forget that self-will can never cast out self-will and that self can never really mortify itself. Happy is the man who is brought to the point of acknowledging his helplessness and powerlessness. He will especially need to deny himself here and cease to expect anything from his own life and strength. He will rather lay himself down in the presence of the Lord as one who is powerless and dead, so that he may really receive the blessing from Him.

It was not Peter who prepared himself for the Day of Pentecost or brought down the Pentecostal blessing from heaven. It was his Lord who did all this for him. His part was to despair of himself and yield himself to his Lord to accomplish in him what He had promised.

It is your part, believer, to deny yourself, to lose your own life, and in the presence of the Lord to sink down in your nothingness and powerlessness. Accustom yourself to set your heart before Him in deep humility, silent patience, and childlike submission. The humility that is prepared to be nothing, the patience that will wait for Him and His time, and the submission that will yield itself wholly so that He may do what seems good are all that you can do to show that you are ready to lose your life.

Jesus summons you to follow Him. Remember how He first sacrificed His will. He laid down His life into the hands of the Father, went down into the grave, and waited until God raised Him to life again. In like manner, you are to be ready to lay down your life in weakness, assured that God will raise it up again in power with the fullness of the Spirit. Forfeit the strength of mere personal efforts and abandon the dominion of your own power. *"Not by might nor by power, but by My Spirit,' says the LORD"* (Zech. 4:6).

DENY YOURSELF DAILY

You of course say at once, "Who is sufficient for these things? Who can sacrifice everything and die and lay down his life utterly as Jesus did? Is such a surrender impossible?" My reply is that it is indeed so. But *"with God all things are possible"* (Matt. 19:26). You cannot literally follow Jesus down into death and the grave. That will always remain beyond your power. Never will our individual selves yield themselves up to death or rest quietly in the grave.

But hear the glad tidings. In Christ you have died and have been buried. The power of His dying, of His willing surrender of His spirit into the hands of the Father, and of His silent resting in the grave works in you. By faith in this working of the spirit and the power of the death and the life of the Lord Jesus, give yourself willingly to lose your life.

For this end, begin to regard the denying of yourself as the first and most necessary work of every day. Accept the message I bring you. The great hindrance in the way of the life of Pentecost is the self-life. Believe in the sinfulness of that life, not because of its gross external sins, but because it sets itself in the place of God. It seeks, pleases, and honors itself more than God.

Recognize your own life as your own worst enemy and as the enemy of God. Begin to see what the full blessing is that Jesus has prepared for you and that He bestowed at Pentecost—namely, His own indwelling. Count nothing too precious or too costly to give as an exchange for this *"pearl of great price"* (Matt. 13:46).

Believer, are you really sincere about being filled with the Spirit of God? Is it your great desire to know what hinders you from obtaining it? Take the word of our Lord and keep it in your heart. Go to Him with it. He is able to make you understand and experience it. It is He who baptizes with the Holy Spirit.

Let everything in you that belongs to self be sacrificed to Him. He, who by His death obtained the Spirit, who prepared Peter for Pentecost in *"the fellowship of His sufferings"* (Phil. 3:10), has your guidance in His hands. Trust your own Jesus. He baptizes with the Spirit beyond doubt or question.

Deny yourself and follow Him. Lose your own life and find His. Let Him impart Himself in the place you have up to this time retained for yourself. From Him there *"will flow rivers of living water"* (John 7:38).

6

HOW THE BLESSING IS OBTAINED BY US

Do not be drunk with wine, in which is dissipation;
but be filled with the Spirit.
—Ephesians 5:18

The command to be filled with the Spirit is just as authoritative as the prohibition not to be drunken with wine. As truly as we are not at liberty to be guilty of the vice are we bound not to be disobedient to the positive command. The same God who calls on us to live in sobriety urges us with equal earnestness to be filled with the Spirit. His command is tantamount to a promise. It is a sure pledge that He Himself will give what He desires us to possess.

With full confidence in this fact, let us ask in all simplicity for the way in which we should live in the will of God, as those who wish to be filled with the Spirit. I suggest to those who really long for this blessing some steps by which they may obtain what is prepared for them.

THE FIRST PRINCIPLE

There are many of God's children who do not believe that the fullness of the Holy Spirit is their inheritance. They imagine that the Day of Pentecost was only the birthday feast of the church and that it was a time of blessing and of power that was not destined to endure. They do not reflect on the command to be filled with the Spirit. The result is that they never seek to receive the full blessing. They remain content with the weak and defective life in which the church of the day exists.

Is this the case with you, my reader? In order to carry on her work in the world, the church requires the full blessing. To please your Lord and to live a life of holiness, joy, and power, you, too, have need of it. To manifest His presence, indwelling, and glory in you, Jesus considers it necessary that you be filled with the Spirit. Believe firmly that the full blessing of Pentecost is a sacred reality. A child of God must have it.

Take time to contemplate it and to allow yourself to be fully possessed by the thought of its glorious significance and power. A firm confidence that the blessing is actually within our reach is the first step toward obtaining it and a powerful impulse in the pursuit.

A SECOND STEP

Admitting that you do not have this blessing is the second step toward it. Perhaps you ask why it should be necessary to cherish this conviction. I will tell you briefly the reason why I consider it of importance.

First, many Christians think that they already have the Holy Spirit, and that all that is required is to be more faithful in their endeavor to know and to obey Him. They think they are already standing in God's grace and that they only need to make a better use of the life they possess. They imagine that they have all that is necessary for continued growth.

On the contrary, it is my deep conviction that such souls are in an unhealthy state and that they have need of a healing. Accordingly, just as the first condition for recovery from disease is the knowledge that one is sick, so it is absolutely necessary for them to acknowledge that they do not walk in the fullness of the Spirit. Being filled with the Spirit is indispensable for them if they are to please God in everything.

Once this first conviction is made thoroughly clear to them, they will be prepared for another consideration—namely, that they ought to acknowledge the guiltiness of their condition. They ought to see that if they have not yet rendered obedience to the command to *"be filled with the Spirit,"* this defect is to be ascribed to sluggishness, self-satisfaction, and unbelief. Once the confession that they have not yet received the full blessing is deeply rooted in them, there will spring from it a stronger impulse to attain it.

IS THIS BLESSING FOR YOU?

I have spoken of those who suppose that the full blessing of Pentecost was only for the first Christian community. Others are willing to acknowledge that it was intended also for the church of later times but still think that all are not entitled to expect it. They might quite reasonably say, "My unfavorable circumstances, my unfortunate disposition, my lack of real ability, and similar difficulties make it impossible for me to realize this ideal. God will not expect this of me. He has not destined me to obtain it."

Do not permit yourself to be deceived by such shallow views. All the members of a body, even to the very least, must be healthy before the body as a whole can be healthy. The indwelling, the fullness of the Spirit is the health of the entire body of Christ. Even if you are the most insignificant member of it, the blessing is for you. In this the Father makes no exceptions.

A great distinction prevails regarding gifts, callings, and circumstances. But there can be no distinction in the love of the Father and His desire to see every one of His children in full health and in the full enjoyment of the Spirit of adoption.

Learn, then, to express and to repeat over again the conviction, "This blessing is for me. My Father desires to have me filled with His Spirit. The blessing lies before me, to be taken with my full consent. I will no longer refuse by unbelief what falls to me as my birthright. With my whole heart, I will say, 'This blessing is for me.'"

OBTAINING THE BLESSING

When a Christian begins to strive for this blessing, he gener-ally makes a variety of efforts to search for the faith, obedience, humility, and submission that are the conditions of obtaining it. When he does not succeed, he is tempted to blame himself. If he does not become utterly discouraged, he rouses himself to still stronger effort and greater zeal.

All this struggling is not without its value and its use, how-ever. It does the very work that the law does. It brings us to the knowledge of our entire powerlessness. It leads us to that despair of ourselves where we become willing to give God the place that belongs to Him. This lesson is entirely indispensable. "I can neither bestow this blessing on myself nor take it. It is God alone who must work it in me."

The blessing of Pentecost is a supernatural gift, a wonderful act of God in the soul. The life of God in every soul is as truly a work of God as when that life was first manifested in Jesus Christ. A Christian can do as little to bring the full life of the Spirit to fruition in his soul as the Virgin Mary did to conceive her supernatural child. (See Luke 1:38.) Like her, he can only receive it as the gift of God.

The impartation of this heavenly blessing is as entirely an act of God as the resurrection of Christ from the dead was His divine work. Christ Jesus had to go down to death and lay aside the life He had in order to receive a new life from God. Likewise, the believer must abandon all power and hope of his own to receive this full blessing as a free gift of divine omnipotence. This acknowledgment of our utter powerlessness, this descent into true self-despair, is indispensable if we wish to enjoy this supreme blessing.

THE PEARL OF GREAT PRICE

The full blessing of Pentecost is to be obtained at no small price. He who desires to have it must sell all and forsake all. Every faculty of our natures, every moment of our lives, and every religious work of our bodies, souls, and spirits must be surrendered to the power of the Spirit of God. In nothing can independent control or independent force have a place. Everything must be under the leading of the Spirit. One must indeed say, "Cost what it may, I am determined to have this blessing." Only the vessel that is utterly empty of everything can be full and overflowing with this living water.

We know that there is often a great gulf between the will and the deed. Even when God has endued the willing, the doing does not always come at once. But it will come wherever a man surrenders himself to the will that God has worked and openly expresses his consent in the presence of God. This, accordingly, is what must be done by the soul who intends to be sincerely ready to part with everything, even though he feels that he has no power to accomplish it.

The selling price is not always paid at the moment of the sale; nevertheless, the purchaser may become the possessor as soon as the sale is concluded and security is given for the payment.

Oh, believer, this very day speak the word, "Cost what it may, I will have this blessing." Jesus is surety that you will have power to abandon everything. Express your decision in the presence of God with confidence and perseverance. Repeat it before your own conscience and say, "I am a purchaser of the pearl of great price. I have offered everything to obtain the full blessing of Pentecost. I have said to God that I must, I will have it. I stand by this decision."

There is a great difference between taking hold of a blessing by faith and the actual experience of it. Christians often become discouraged when they do not at once experience the feeling and the enjoyment of what is promised them. When you have said that you forsake all and count it but loss for the full blessing of Pentecost, then from that moment you have to believe that He receives your offer and that He bestows on you the fullness of the Spirit.

Yet it may easily be that you cannot at that time trace any noticeable change in your experience. It is as if everything in you remained in its old condition. Now, however, is the very time to persevere in faith. Learn by faith to be as sure as if you had seen it written in heaven that God has accepted your surrender of everything as a certain and completed transaction.

In faith look on yourself as a person who is known to God as one who has sold everything to obtain this heavenly treasure. Believe that God has given you the fullness of the Spirit. Regard yourself as on the way to knowing the full blessing in feeling as well as in experience. Believe that God will order this blessing to break forth and be revealed in you. In faith let your life be a life of joyful thanksgiving and expectation. God will not disappoint you.

WAIT FOR THE MANIFESTATION

Faith must lead you to the actual inheritance of the promise and to the experience and enjoyment of it. Do not rest content with a belief that does not lead to experience. Rest in God by faith in the full assurance that He can make Himself known to you in a manner that is truly divine. At times the whole process may appear to you too great and too wonderful and really impossible.

Do not be afraid. The more clearly you discern the fact that you have said to God that He may take you and fill you with His Holy Spirit, the more you will feel what a miracle of the grace of God it is. There may be in you things you are not aware of that hinder the breaking forth of the blessing. God is bent on putting them aside. Let them be consumed in the fire. Let them be annihilated in the flame of God's countenance and His love. Let your expectation be fixed on the Lord your God.

He who raised up the dead Jesus to the life of glory will just as miraculously bring this heavenly blessing to fruition in you. Then you may be filled with the Holy Spirit and know, not by reasoning but by experience, that you have actually received the Holy Spirit.

God desires to make you full of the Holy Spirit. He desires to have your whole nature and life under the power of the Holy Spirit. He asks if you really desire to have it. Let there be in your answer no uncertainty, but let all that is within you cry out, "Yes, Lord, with all my heart." Let this promise of your God become the chief element in your life, the most precious, the only thing you seek. Do not be content to think and pray over it, but this very day enter into a transaction with God that will allow no doubt concerning the choice you have made.

When you have made this choice, cleave firmly to the faith that expects this blessing as a miracle of divine omnipotence. The more earnestly you exercise that faith, the more it will teach you that your heart must be entirely emptied and set free from every fetter, to be filled with the Spirit. You may take it for granted that it will surely come.

7

HOW THE BLESSING MAY
BE STRENGTHENED

This blessing of Pentecost is entrusted to us as a talent that must be used, and only by use does it become strong. The Lord Jesus, after He was baptized with the Holy Spirit, was perfected by obedience and submission to the leading of the Spirit. Likewise, the Christian who has received the blessing of Pentecost must guard safely the deposit entrusted to him.

When we inquire how we can grow spiritually, Scripture points us to the fact that we can confidently entrust our spiritual life to the Lord. *"He is able to keep what I have committed to Him....That good thing which was committed to you, keep by the Holy Spirit who dwells in us"* (2 Tim. 1:12, 14). After saying, *"Keep yourselves in the love of God"* (Jude 21), Jude added the doxology, *"To Him who is able to keep you...be glory"* (vv. 24–25).

The main secret of success in the development of the blessing is the exercise of a humble dependence on the Lord who keeps us and on the Spirit by whom we ourselves are kept in close fellowship with Him. This blessing, as the manna that fell in the wilderness, must be renewed from heaven every day. The new heavenly life, as with the life we live on earth, must be drawn in every moment in sustaining fresh air from without and from above. Let us see how this ever-abiding, uninterrupted keeping takes place.

Jesus is the Keeper of Israel. This is His name and His work. God not only created the world but also keeps and upholds it. Jesus is not content with merely giving the blessing of Pentecost. He will also maintain it every moment. The Holy Spirit is not a power that in any sense is subordinate to us, entrusted to us, or to be used by us. He is an energizing power that is over and above us, carrying forward His work from moment to moment. Our right place and our proper attitude must always be that of the deepest dependence in our own nothingness and powerlessness. Our chief concern is to let Jesus do His work within us.

As long as the soul does not discern this truth, there will always be a certain dread of receiving the full blessing. Such a one will be inclined to say, "I will not be able to continue in that holy life. I will not be able to dwell on such a lofty plane all the time." But these thoughts only show what a feeble grasp one has of the great reality. When Jesus comes by the Spirit to dwell in my heart and to live in me, He will actually work out the maintenance of the blessing and regard my whole inner life as His special care.

The joy of the blessing of Pentecost, while it can never be relieved of the necessity of watchfulness, is a life that is freed from anxiety and ought to be characterized by continual gladness. The Lord has come into His holy temple. There He will abide and work out everything. He desires only that the soul will know and honor Him as its faithful Shepherd and Almighty Keeper.

JESUS WILL KEEP THE BLESSING

The law that prevails at every stage in the progress of the kingdom of God is, *"According to your faith let it be to you"* (Matt. 9:29). The faith that you had when you first received the Lord Jesus was as small as a grain of mustard seed. It must, in the course of the Christian life, become so enlarged that it will see and enjoy more of the fullness that is in the Lord.

Paul wrote to the Galatians, *"It is no longer I who live, but Christ lives in me; and the life which I now live in the flesh I live by faith in the Son of God"* (Gal. 2:20). His faith was as broad and boundless as were the needs of his life and work.

In everything and at all times, without ceasing, he trusted in Jesus to do all. Paul's faith was as wide and abundant as the energy that flows from Jesus. He had given his whole life to Jesus, and he himself lived no longer. By a continuous and unrestricted faith, he gave Jesus the liberty of energizing his life without ceasing and without limitation.

The fullness of the Spirit is not a gift that is given once for all as a part of the heavenly life. Rather, it is a constantly flowing stream of the river of the water of life that issues from beneath the throne of God and of the Lamb (Rev. 22:1). It is an uninterrupted communication of the life and the love of Jesus, the most personal and intimate association of the Lord with His own on the earth. Jesus will certainly do His work of keeping if faith discerns this truth and cleaves to it with joy.

CLOSER FELLOWSHIP WITH JESUS

Jesus keeps this blessing in fellowship with Himself. The single aim of the blessing of Pentecost is to reveal Jesus as Savior, so that He may exhibit His power to redeem souls in us and by us here in the world. The Spirit did not come merely to occupy the place of Jesus, but to unite the disciples with their Lord more completely than when He was on earth.

The power from on high did not come as a power that they were henceforth to consider as their own. The power was inseparably bound up with the Lord Jesus and the Holy Spirit. Every operation of the power was a direct working of God in them.

The fellowship that the disciples had with Jesus on earth— following Him, receiving His teaching, doing His will, and participating in His suffering—was still to be their experience, only in greater measure.

It is no different with us. The Spirit in us will always glorify Jesus and make it known that He alone is to be Lord. Close communion with God in the inner chamber, faithfulness in searching His Word and seeking to know His will in the Scriptures, sacrificing time and business to bring us into touch with the Savior are all indispensable for the enrichment of the blessing. He who loves His fellowship above everything will have the experience of His keeping.

FOR THE OBEDIENT

When the Lord Jesus promised to send the Holy Spirit, He said three times that the blessing was for the obedient. *"If you love Me, keep My commandments. And I will pray the Father, and He will give you another Helper, that He may abide with you forever"* (John 14:15–16). Peter spoke of *"the Holy Spirit whom God has given to those who obey Him"* (Acts 5:32).

Of our Lord Himself we read that He *"became obedient to the point of death....Therefore God also has highly exalted Him"* (Phil. 2:8–9). Obedience is what God demands. Obedience attains what was lost by the Fall. Jesus came to restore the power of obedience. It is His own life. Apart from obedience, the blessing of Pentecost can neither come nor abide.

There are two kinds of obedience. One that is very defective is like that of the disciples prior to Pentecost. They desired from the heart to do what the Lord said, but they did not have the power. Yet the Lord accounted their desire and purpose as obedience. On the other hand, there is a more abundant life that comes with the fullness of the Spirit, where new power is given for full obedience.

The characteristic of the full blessing of Pentecost is a surrender to obedience in the minutest details. To listen to the voice of Jesus Himself, to the voice of the Spirit, and to the voice of conscience is the way Jesus leads us. The method of making the life of Pentecost within us sure and strong is to know Jesus, to love Him, and to receive Him in the aspect that made Him well-pleasing to the Father—namely, as the Obedient One.

The exercise of this obedience gives the soul a wonderful firmness, confidence, and power to trust God and to expect all from Him. A strong will is necessary for a strong faith, and it is in obedience that the will is strengthened to trust God to the uttermost. This is the only way in which the Lord can lead us to ever richer blessing.

ONE BODY, ONE SPIRIT

At the outset of his seeking the full blessing, a Christian may think primarily of himself. Even after he receives the blessing as a new experience, he is still rather disposed to see merely how he can keep it safely for himself. But very speedily the Spirit will teach him that a member of the body cannot enjoy the flow of healthy life in a state of separation from others. He begins to understand that there is one body and one Spirit. The unity of the body must be realized to enjoy the fullness of the Spirit.

This principle teaches us some very important lessons about the condition in which the blessing should be maintained. All that you have belongs to others and must be used for their service. All that they have belongs to you and is indispensable for you. The Spirit of the body of the Lord can work effectively only when the members of it work in unison.

You should confess to others what the Lord has done for you, ask their intercession, seek their fellowship, and help them with what the Lord has given you. You should take to heart the unhappy condition of the enfeebled Christian church in our days. It should not be done in the spirit of judgment or bitterness, but rather in the spirit of humility and prayer.

Jesus will teach you what is meant by the saying that love is the greatest. By the very intensity of your surrender to the welfare of His church, He will increase the blessing in you.

The very name of Jesus Christ involves entire consecration to God's work of rescuing souls. It was for this end that He lived on earth and for this cause that He lives in heaven. How can anyone ever dream of having the Spirit of Christ except as a Spirit that aims at the work of God and the salvation of souls? It is an impossibility. Therefore, from the outset we must keep these two aspects of the Spirit's operation closely knit together. What the Spirit works in us is for the sake of what He works by us. We must present ourselves to be used by the Spirit to do His work.

ONE MORE THOUGHT

Whenever mention is made of Jesus as our Keeper, it is often difficult to believe that we who are on the earth can really know ourselves to be always, without interruption, in His hands and under His power. How much clearer and more glorious the truth becomes when the Spirit reveals to us that Christ is in us. He is in us, not only as a tenant in a house or as water in a glass, but rather as the soul is in the body, moving every part and never being separated from each other.

Yes, Christ dwells in us, penetrating our entire natures with His nature. The Holy Spirit came for the purpose of making Jesus deeply present within us. The sun is high in the firmament above me and yet, by its heat, penetrates my bones and marrow and quickens my whole life. Likewise, the Lord Jesus, who is exalted high in heaven, penetrates my whole nature by His Spirit until all my willing, thinking, and feeling are moved by Him.

Once this fact is fully grasped, we no longer think of an external keeping through a person outside of us in heaven. We become convinced that our lives are quickened by One who, in a divine manner, occupies the heart. Then we see how natural, how certain, and how blessed it is that the indwelling Jesus keeps the blessing and always maintains the fullness of the Spirit.

Brothers and sisters, is there anyone among you who is longing for this life in the fullness of blessing, yet is afraid to enter into it because he does not know how to persevere? Jesus will make this blessing continuous and sure. Is there any one of you who longs for it and cannot understand where the secret lies? The blessing is this: as Jesus Christ was with His disciples daily in bodily fashion, so He will, by His Spirit, daily live His life in you. No one can fully understand how things look on the top of a mountain until he himself has been there.

Although you do not understand everything, believe that the Lord Jesus has sent His Spirit with no other purpose than to keep you in His divine power. Trust Him for this. Let all burdens be laid aside to receive this blessing from Him as a fountain that He Himself will cause to spring up in you unto everlasting life.

8

HOW YOUR BLESSING MAY BE INCREASED

He who believes in Me shall never thirst.
—John 6:35

*He who believes in Me,…out of his heart will
flow rivers of living water.*
—John 7:38

Can the full blessing of Pentecost be still further increased?
Can anything that is full become still fuller? Yes, undoubtedly.

It can become so full that it always overflows, especially this blessing of Pentecost.

The above words of our blessed Lord Jesus point us to a double blessing. First, Jesus says that he who believes in Him will never thirst. He will always have the satisfaction of having his needs met. Then, He speaks of something that is grander and more glorious. Whoever believes in Him, *"out of his heart will flow rivers of living water"* to quench the thirst of others. It is the distinction between full and overflowing. A vessel may be full and yet have nothing left over for others. When it remains full and has something for others, there must be in it an over-brimming, ever-flowing supply. This is what our Lord promises to His believing disciples. At the outset, faith in Him gives them the blessing that they will never thirst. But as they advance and become stronger in the faith, it makes them a fountain of water out of which streams flow to others. The Spirit who at first only fills us will overflow out of us to souls around us.

The rivers of living water can be compared with many fountains on earth. When we begin to open them, the stream is weak. The more the water is used, and the more deeply the source is opened up, the stronger the water flows. In the realm of the spiritual life, let us discover what is necessary to secure the fullness of the Spirit constantly flowing from us. Several simple steps may help us in reaching this knowledge.

HOLD FAST TO WHAT YOU HAVE

First, see to it that you do not misunderstand the blessing God has given you. Be sure that you do not form any wrong ideas of what the full blessing is. Do not imagine that the joy and power of Pentecost must be felt and seen immediately. No, the church at present is in a dead-and-alive condition, and restoration often comes slowly.

At first, one receives the full blessing only as a seed. The quickened soul has longed for it; he has surrendered himself unreservedly for it; he has believed in silence that God has accepted his consecration and fulfilled His promise. In this faith he goes on his way, silent and happy, saying to himself, "The blessing of the fullness of the Spirit is for me."

But the actual experiences of the blessing did not come as he had anticipated. The result was that he began to fear that his surrender was not a reality, only a transient emotion. He feared the real blessing was something greater and more powerful than he had yet received. The result is that very soon the blessing becomes less instead of greater. Through discouragement, he moves farther back rather than forward.

The cause of this condition is simply lack of faith. We are bent on judging God and His work in us by sight and feeling. We forget that the whole process is the work of faith. Even in its highest revelations in Christians who have made the greatest progress, faith rests not on what is to be seen of the work of God or on the experiences of it, but on the work of God as spiritual, invisible, deeply hidden, and inconceivable.

Do you desire in this time of discouragement to return to the true life according to the promise? My advice is this: if you know that you have given yourself to God with a perfect heart, then rest in silence before Him and hold fast your integrity. Do this, and you will know God.

If you are sure that you have set yourself before God as an empty, purified vessel, then continue to regard yourself so and keep silent before Him. If you have believed that God has received you to fill you as a purified vessel—purified through Jesus Christ and by your entire surrender to Him—then abide in this attitude day by day. You may expect the blessing to grow and begin to flow. *"Whoever believes…will not be put to shame"* (Rom. 9:33).

PERSEVERE IN SELF-DENIAL

In your surrender you have said in truth and uprightness that you are prepared to sacrifice and forsake everything in order to win this pearl of the kingdom of heaven. This consecration was acceptable to God. But you have not yet fully understood the importance of the words you have used. The Lord still has much to teach you concerning what the individual self is, how deeply rooted it is in your nature, and how utterly corrupt as well as deeply hidden it is.

Be willing to make room for the Spirit by a constant, daily denial of the self-life. You may be sure that He will always be willing to come and fill the empty place. You have forsaken and sacrificed everything as far as you know, but keep your mind open to the teaching of the Spirit. He will lead you farther on and let you see that when the sacrifice of everything becomes the rule in His church, then the blessing will again break forth like an overflowing stream.

It is surprising how sometimes a very little thing may hinder the continuance in the increase of the blessing. It may, for example, be a little disagreement between friends, where they are not willing to forgive and bear with one another at once according to the law of Christ. Or it may be some unobserved yielding to oversensitiveness or to ambition that is not prepared to take the lowest place. Or it may be the possession or use of earthly property as if it were our own.

It may also be in connection with things that are lawful and in themselves innocent, which, however, do not harmonize with us in our claim of being led by the Spirit of God. For here, like the Lord Jesus in His poverty, we are bound to show that the heavenly portion we possess is itself sufficient to satisfy all our desires. Or it may be in connection with questionable things, in which we give way too easily to the lust of the flesh.

Christian, do you really desire to enjoy the full measure of the blessing of the Spirit? Then, before temptation comes, train yourself to understand the fundamental law of the imitation of Jesus and of full discipleship, and forsake all. Allow yourself to be strengthened and drawn into the observance of it by the sure promise of the "hundredfold in this life." (See Matthew 19:29.) A full blessing will be given you, a measure *"shaken together, and running over"* (Luke 6:38).

SACRIFICE AND GIVING

"God is love" (1 John 4:8). His whole being is nothing but a surrender of Himself in love to be the life of the creature and to make the creature participate in His holiness and blessedness. He blesses and serves all who live. His glory as God is that He puts all that He has at the disposal of His creatures.

Jesus Christ is the Son of God's love, the Bearer, Bringer, and Dispenser of the love. What God is as invisible in heaven,

He was as visible on earth. He came, He lived, He suffered, and He died only to glorify the Father, to let it be seen how glorious the Father is in His love. He came to show that in the Godhead there is no other purpose than to bless men, to make them happy, and to show that the highest honor and blessedness of any being is to give and to sacrifice.

The Holy Spirit came as the Spirit of the Father and the Son to make us partakers of this divine nature. The Spirit pours out the love of God in our hearts (Rom. 5:5) to secure the indwelling of the Son and His love to such an extent that Christ may be formed within us, and our whole inner man will bear the imprint of His likeness.

Hence, when any soul seeks and receives the fullness of the Spirit, is it not perfectly evident that he can enjoy this blessing only as he is prepared to give himself to a life in the service of love? The Spirit comes to expel the life of self and self-seeking. The fullness of the Spirit presupposes a willingness to consecrate ourselves to the blessing of others as the servants of all. The Spirit is the outflowing of the life of God. If we will only yield ourselves to Him, He will become the river of living water, flowing from the depths of our hearts.

Christian, if you want the blessing increased, begin to live only so that the love of God may work through you. Love everyone around you with the love of God that is in you through the Spirit. Love the children of God cordially, even the weakest and most perverse. Exercise and exhibit your love in every possible way. Love the unsaved. Present yourself to the Spirit to love Him. Then love will constrain you to speak, to work, to give, and to pray.

If there is no open door for working, or if you do not have the strength for it, the door of prayer is always open, and power can be obtained at the mercy seat. Embrace the whole world in your love, because Christ, who is in your heart, belongs also to the unsaved. The Spirit is the power of Christ for redeeming them. Like God and Jesus and the Spirit, live wholly to bless others. Then the blessing will stream forth and become overflowing.

LET JESUS CHRIST BE EVERYTHING

You know what the Scripture says: *"All the promises of God in Him are Yes, and in Him Amen, to the glory of God through us"* (2 Cor. 1:20). When the Lord spoke of *"rivers of living water,"* He connected the promise with faith in Himself: *"He who believes in Me,…out of his heart will flow rivers."* If we only understood that word *"believes"* rightly, we would require no other answer than this to the question as to how the blessing may be increased.

Faith is primarily a seeing by the Spirit that Jesus is nothing but a flowing fountain of divine love. The Spirit Himself always flows from Him as the Bearer of the life that this love brings and that always streams forth in love. Then it is an embracing of the promise, a taking hold of the blessing as it is provided in Christ, a resting in the certainty of it, and a thanking God for what He is yet to do.

Thereafter, faith is keeping the soul open so that Christ can come in with the blessing, take possession, and fill all. Faith becomes the most fervent and unbroken communion between the soul and Christ, who obtains His place and is enthroned in the heart.

Learn the lesson that, if you believe, you will see the glory of God. Let every doubt, every weakness, every temptation find you trusting, rejoicing, and counting on Jesus always to work all in you.

A believer can encounter and strive against sin in two ways. One is to endeavor to ward it off with all his might, seeking his strength in the Word and in prayer. In this form of conflict, we use the power of the will. The other is to turn at the very moment of the temptation to the Lord Jesus in the silent exercise of faith and say to Him, "Lord, I have no strength. You are my Keeper."

This is the method of faith. *"This is the victory that has overcome the world; our faith"* (1 John 5:4). Jesus, who is in Himself the one thing needed, can maintain the work of His Spirit in us. When we exercise faith without ceasing, the blessing will flow in us without ceasing.

Christ must be all to us every moment. It is of no avail to me that I have life on earth unless that life is renewed every moment by my breathing fresh air. Similarly, God must actually renew and strengthen the divine life in me every moment. He does this for me in my union with Christ. Christ is simply the fullness of God, the life of God, and the love of God prepared for us and communicating themselves to us. The Spirit is simply the fullness of Christ, the life of Christ, and the self-communicating love of Christ surrounding us as the air surrounds the body.

Let us believe that we are in Christ, who surrounds us in His heavenly power, longing to make the rivers of His Spirit flow forth through us. Let us endeavor to obtain hearts filled with the joyful assurance that the almighty Lord will fulfill His word with power. Our only choice is to see Him, to rejoice in Him, to sacrifice all for Him. Then His word will become true: *"He who believes in Me,...out of his heart will flow rivers of living water."*

9

IN SEARCH OF THE FULL MANIFESTATION

For this reason I bow my knees to the Father
of our Lord Jesus Christ.
—Ephesians 3:14

Paul, in writing to the church at Ephesus, wished to make it clear to them that he desired several things for their spiritual growth. Thus, he wrote, "I bow my knees to the Father," for the following reasons:

- "*That He would grant you...to be strengthened with might through His Spirit in the inner man*" (Eph. 3:16).

- "*That Christ may dwell in your hearts through faith*" (v. 17).

- "*That you, being rooted and grounded in love, may...know the love of Christ which passes knowledge*" (vv. 17–19).

- "*That you may be filled with all the fullness of God*" (v. 19).

Every blessing God gives is like a seed with the power of an indissoluble life hidden in it. Do not imagine that to be filled with the Spirit is a condition of perfection that leaves nothing more to be desired. In no sense can this be true. After the Lord Jesus was filled with the Spirit at His baptism, He had to go forth to be still further perfected by temptations and the learning of obedience. (See Matthew 4:1–11.)

When the disciples were filled with the Spirit on the Day of Pentecost, this equipping with "*power from on high*" (Luke 24:49) was given to them so that they might have victory over sin in their own lives.

The Spirit is the Spirit of truth, and He must guide us into it (John 16:13). He will lead us into the eternal purpose of God, into the knowledge of Christ, into true holiness, and into full fellowship with God. The fullness of the Spirit is simply the full preparation for living and working as a child of God.

When we consider the matter from this point of view, we see at a glance how entirely indispensable it is for every child of God to aim at obtaining this blessing. We also understand why Paul offered this prayer on behalf of all believers without distinction. He did not regard it as a spiritual distinction or special luxury that was intended only for those who were prominent or favored among the children of God. No, he prayed for all, without distinction, who at their conversion had by faith received the Holy Spirit.

His request was that, by the special work of the Spirit, God would bring them to their true destiny—to be *"filled with all the fullness of God"* (Eph. 3:19). Paul's prayer is regarded as one of the most glorious representations of what the life of a Christian ought to be. Let us endeavor to learn what the full revelation and manifestation of this blessing of the Spirit may become.

STRENGTHENED WITH POWER

That these Christians had received the Spirit when they believed in Christ is clear from a previous statement in the epistle. But Paul saw that they did not yet know or have all that the Spirit could do for them. He realized there was a danger that, by their ignorance, they might make no further progress.

Hence he bowed his knees and prayed without ceasing on their behalf, that the Father would strengthen them with might by His Spirit in the inner man. This powerful strengthening with the Spirit is equivalent to being filled with the Spirit, and it is indeed another aspect of this same blessing. It is the indispensable condition of a healthy, growing, and fruitful life.

Paul prayed that the Father would grant this gift. He asked for a new, definite operation of God. He requested that God would do this according to the riches of His glory. It is surely not any common, trifling thing that he asked. He desired that God would remember and bring into play all the riches of His grace and strengthen these believers with might by His Spirit in the inner man.

Oh, Christian, learn at this point that your life daily depends on God's will, on God's grace, and on God's omnipotence. Yes, every moment God must work in your inner life and strengthen you by His Spirit; otherwise, you cannot live as He desires you to live. Just as no creature in the natural world can exist for a moment if God does not work in it to sustain its life, so the gift of the Holy Spirit is the pledge that God Himself is to work everything in us from moment to moment.

Learn to know your entire, blessed dependence on God. Recognize the claim you have on Him as your heavenly Father to begin in you a life in the mighty strengthening of the Spirit and to maintain it without the interruption of a single moment.

Paul told these believers what he prayed for on their behalf in order that they might know what they had need of and ask for it themselves. Expect everything from God alone. Bow your knees, ask, and expect from the Father His manifestation to you of the riches of His glory. Ask and expect that He will strengthen you with might by His Spirit who is already in you as an unknown, hidden, and slumbering seed.

Let this become the desire and confidence of your soul: "God will fill me with the Spirit; God will strengthen me through the Spirit with His almighty energy." Let your whole life be daily permeated by this prayer and this expectation.

WHAT IS GOD'S AIM?

This is the glorious fruit of the divine strengthening with might in the inner man by the Spirit. The great work of the Father in eternity is to bring forth the Son.

In Him alone the good pleasure of God is realized. The Father can have no fellowship with the creature except through the Son. He can have no joy in it except as He beholds His Son in it. His great work in redemption is to reveal His Son in us so that our lives will be visible expressions of the life of Jesus.

This indwelling of Christ is not like that of a man who abides in a house and is in no sense identified with it. No, His indwelling is a possession of our hearts that is truly divine, quickening, and penetrating our innermost being with His life. The Father strengthens us inwardly with might by His Spirit (Eph. 3:16), so that the Spirit animates our wills and brings them, like the will of Jesus, into entire sympathy with His own.

The result is that our hearts, like the heart of Jesus, then bow before Him in humility and surrender, seeking only His honor. Our entire souls thrill with desire and love for Jesus. This inward renewal makes the heart fit to be a dwelling place of the Lord. By the Spirit He is revealed within us, and we come to know that He is actually in us as our Life in a deep, divine unity—He is one with us.

Believer, God longs to see Jesus in you. He is prepared to work mightily in you so that Christ may dwell in you. The Spirit has come, and the Father is willing to work mightily by Him so that the living presence of His Son may always abide in you. Jesus loves you dearly and longs intensely for you. He cannot rest until He makes His abode in your heart. This is the supreme blessing that the fullness of the Spirit brings you.

By faith, you receive and know the indwelling of the Spirit and the operation of the Father by Him. By faith, which discerns invisible things as clearly as the sun, you receive and know the living Jesus in your heart. As constantly as He was with His disciples on earth—yes, even more constantly than with them—He will be in you and will grant you the enjoyment of His presence and His love.

Dear reader, pray that the Father will strengthen you with might by the Spirit and open your heart for the fullness of the Spirit. Then at last you will know what it means to have Christ dwelling in your heart by faith.

LOVE IS...

"*That you, being rooted and grounded in love, may...know the love of Christ which passes knowledge*" (Eph. 3:17–19). Here is the glorious fruit of the indwelling of Christ in the heart. By the Spirit, the love of God is poured out in the heart (Rom. 5:5). By Christ, who dwells in the heart, the love with which God loved Him comes into us. Just as life in God—between Father, Son, and Spirit—is only infinite love, so the life of Christ in us is nothing but love.

Thus we become "*rooted and grounded in love.*" We are planted in the soil of love, and we strike our roots into heavenly love; henceforth, we have our being in it and draw our strength from it. Love is the supreme element in our spiritual lives. The Spirit in us and the Son in us bring us nothing but the love of God.

Love is the first and the chief among the streams of living water that are to flow from us.

"*Love is the fulfillment of the law*"; it "*does no harm to a neighbor*" (Rom. 13:10). It "*does not seek it own*" (1 Cor. 13:5). It causes us to *"lay down our lives for the brethren"* (1 John 3:16). Our hearts become ever larger and larger.

Our friends, our enemies, the children of God, and the children of the world are worthy to be loved. Those who are the hated, the ransomed and the lost, the world as a whole, and every individual creature in particular are all embraced in the love of God.

Our happiness lies in sacrificing our honor, our advantage, and our comfort in favor of others. Love takes no account of sacrifice. It is blessed to love.

We are able to love only because the Father, with His Spirit, works mightily within us and because His Son dwells in us. He, who is crucified love, has filled our hearts completely with Himself. We are rooted in love. In accordance with the nature of the root, God produces the fruit—love.

Dear readers, listen to the Word: *"God is love"* (1 John 4:8). He has provided everything so that you may know love fully. It is with this aim that Christ desires to have your whole hearts. Begin to pray that the Father will strengthen you with might by the Spirit, and that you may know the love of Christ.

FILLED WITH THE FULLNESS

Filled with the fullness of God—this is the experience to which the fullness of the Spirit is intended to bring us and will bring us.

God has made provisions for our enlightenment. In Christ Jesus we see a man full of God, a man who was perfected by suffering and obedience, filled with all the fullness of God. He was a man, who in the solitariness and poverty of an ordinary human life, with all its needs and infirmities, has nevertheless let us see on earth the life enjoyed by the inhabitants of heaven. The will and the honor, the love and the service of God were always visible in Him. God was everything to Him.

When God called the world into existence, it was in order that it might reveal Him. In it His wisdom, might, and goodness were to dwell and be visibly manifested. We say continually that nature is full of God. God can be seen in everything by the believing eye. The seraphim sing, and *"the whole earth is full of His glory"* (Isa. 6:3). When God created man after His image, it was in order that He Himself might be seen in man, that man would simply serve as a reflection of His likeness. The image of a man never serves any other purpose than to represent the man. As the image of God, man was destined simply to receive the glory of God in his own life, to bear it and make it visible. Man was to be full of God.

This divine purpose has been frustrated by sin. Instead of being full of God, man became full of himself and the world. Sin has blinded us to such an extent that it appears an impossibility ever to become full of God again. Even many Christians see nothing desirable in this fullness. Yet Jesus came to redeem us and bring us back to this blessing. God is prepared to work mightily within us by His Spirit. This is no less the result for which the Son of God desires to dwell in our hearts and which He will bring to accomplishment.

Yes, this is the highest aim of the Pentecostal blessing. To attain this, we can count on the Spirit to make sure of our reaching it. He will open the way for us and guide us in it. He will work in us the deep humility of Jesus, who always said, "I *can of Myself do nothing*" (John 5:30); "*not to do My own will*" (John 6:38); "*the words that I speak to you I do not speak on My own authority*" (John 14:10). Amid this self-emptying and sense of dependence, He will work in us the assurance and the experience that, for the soul that is nothing, God is surely *all*. By our faith He will reveal Jesus to us, who is full of God. He will cause us to be rooted in the love in which God gives all, and we will take God as all. Thus it will be with us as with Jesus: man is nothing, and God's honor, His will, His love, and His power are everything.

Christian, I beg of you by the love of God not to say that this is too high an experience for you or that it is not for you. No, it is in truth the will of God concerning you—the will of His commandment and of His promise. He Himself will work it out. Today, in humility and faith, take this word, "*Filled with all the fullness of God*" (Eph. 3:19), as the purpose and the watchword of your life, and see what it will do for you.

It will become to you a mighty lever to raise you out of the self-seeking that is quite content with only being prepared for blessing. It will urge you to enter into and become firmly rooted in the love of God. It will convince you that nothing less than Christ Himself dwelling in your heart can keep such a love abiding in you. It will make the fullness of God a reality within you.

Go down on your knees and summon to your aid the wealth of God's glory. Continue to do this until your heart is able to utter the response, "Yes, being filled with the fullness of God is what my God has prepared for me."

With this glorious prospect before you, join with the apostle in the doxology: "*Now to Him who is able to do exceedingly abundantly above all that we ask or think, according to the power that works in us* [the power of His might], *to Him be glory"* (Eph. 3:20–21). Desire nothing less than these riches of the glory of God. Today, if you have never done it before, *"be filled with all the fullness of God"* (v. 19).

When God said to Abraham, *"I am God Almighty"* (Gen. 35:11), He invited him to trust His omnipotence to fulfill His promise. When Jesus went down into the grave, it was in the faith that God's omnipotence could lift Him to the throne of His glory. That same omnipotence waits to work out God's purpose in those who believe in Him to do so. Let our hearts say, *"Now to Him who is able to do exceedingly abundantly above all that we ask or think,...to Him be glory"* (Eph. 3:20–21).

10

HOW FULLY IT IS ASSURED TO US BY GOD

If you then, being evil, know how to give good gifts to your children, how much more will your heavenly Father give the Holy Spirit to those who ask Him!
—Luke 11:13

When Jairus came to the Lord Jesus to entreat His help for his dying daughter, he had already learned that she had died. Jesus said to him, *"Do not be afraid; only believe"* (Luke 8:50). Face to face with a trial in which man was utterly helpless, the

Lord called on him to put his trust in Him. One thing could help him: *"Only believe."*

Thousands of times this word has been the strength of God's children. Where man was concerned, all hope was lost and success appeared to be impossible. Here again, in seeking the full Pentecostal blessing, we have need of this word. The wonder-working power of God can make this exceeding grace a reality within us. Be silent before God. Hear the voice of Jesus saying to us, *"'Do not be afraid; only believe.' God will do it for you."*

God will give the Holy Spirit to those who ask Him much more readily than an earthly father will give his children bread. We must have firm confidence in the Father to give His child His full heritage. *"God is Spirit"* (John 4:24). He desires in His eternal love to obtain full possession of us, but He can do this in no other manner than by giving us His Spirit. Child of God, as surely as He is God, He will fill you with His Holy Spirit.

Without this faith you will never succeed in your quest for this blessing. This faith will give you the victory over every difficulty. Therefore, *"do not be afraid; only believe"* (Luke 8:50). Hear the voice of Jesus: *"Did I not say to you that if you would believe you would see the glory of God?"* (John 11:40).

HOW DOES THIS BLESSING COME?

Preliminary questions arise at once in connection with this subject and tempt us to understand everything about it before we expect the blessing.

The first question is, Where does this blessing come from, from within or from above? Some earnest Christians will say at once that it must come from within. The Holy Spirit descended on the earth on the Day of Pentecost and was given to the Christian community. At the moment of conversion, He comes into our hearts. Therefore, we no longer have to pray that He may be given to us. We have simply to recognize and use what we already have. We do not have to seek more of the Spirit because we have Him in the fullness of the gift as it is. It is rather the Holy Spirit who must have more of us. As we yield ourselves entirely to Him, He will entirely fill us from within. The fountain of living water is already there. It has only to be open and every obstruction cleared, and the water will stream forth from within.

On the other hand, a few may say, "No, it must come from above." When, on the arrival of the Day of Pentecost, the Father freely gave the Spirit, He did not give Him away beyond His own control. The fullness of the Spirit still remains in God. God gives nothing apart from Himself to work without or independently of His will. He Himself works only through the Spirit, and every new and greater manifestation of the Spirit's power comes directly from above. Long after the Day of Pentecost, the Spirit came down again from heaven at Samaria and Caesarea. In His fullness He is in heaven still, and it is from God in heaven that the fullness of the Spirit is to be waited for.

Christian, pray. Do not linger until by reasonings of your own you have decided which of these representations is the right one. God can bless people in both ways. When the Flood came, all the fountains of the abyss were broken up and the floodgates of heaven were opened. It came simultaneously from beneath and from above. God is prepared to bless people in both of these methods. He desires to teach us to know and honor the

Spirit who is already within us. He desires to bring us to wait on Himself in a spirit of utter dependence.

I entreat you not to allow yourself to be held back by such a question as this. God understands your petition. He knows what you need. Believe that God is prepared to fill you with His Spirit. Let your faith look up to Him with unceasing prayer and confidence, and He will give the blessing.

The other question is, Does this blessing come gradually or at once? Will it manifest itself in the shape of a silent, unobserved increase of the grace of the Spirit or as a momentary, immediate outpouring of His power? It must suffice for me to say here again that God has already sent this blessing in both modes and will continue to do so.

There must be a definite resolution, however, to place one's whole life unreservedly under the control of the Spirit and a conviction of faith that God has accepted this surrender. In the majority of cases, this is done at once. Perhaps after a long course of seeking and praying, the soul must come to the place at which it will present itself to God for this blessing in one definite, irrevocable act and believe that the offering is then sanctified and accepted on the altar. Whether the experience of the blessing comes at once and with power or quietly and gradually, the soul must maintain its act of self-dedication and simply look to God to do His own work.

Thus, in dealing with all such questions, the chief concern is this: "*Only believe*" (Luke 8:50), and rest in the faithfulness of God. Hold fast this one principle: God has given us a promise that He will fill us with His Spirit. It is His work to make His promise an accomplished fact. Thank God for the promise even as you would thank Him for the fulfillment of it. In the promise, God has already pledged Himself to you. Rejoice in Him and in His faithfulness. Do not be held back by any questions whatsoever. Set your heart on what God will do and on Him from whom the blessing must come. The result will be certain and glorious.

MORE OF THE SPIRIT

It is sad that so many in the church are content with things just as they are. They have no desire to know more of this seeking for the reality of the Spirit's power. They point to the present purity of doctrine, to the prevailing earnestness of preaching, to the generous gifts that are made for the maintenance of religious works and the enterprises of philanthropy. They look to the interest manifested in education and missions, and they say that it is better to give God thanks for the good we see around us. Such people would condemn the language of Laodicea and would refuse to say that they were *"rich, and increased with goods, and [had] need of nothing"* (Rev. 3:17 KJV).

Yet there are some traces of this spirit in what they say. They do not consider the command to be filled with the Spirit. They have forgotten the command to prophesy to the Spirit and say, *"Come from the four winds, O breath, and breathe on these slain, that they may live"* (Ezek. 37:9). When you speak of these things, you will receive little encouragement from these people. They do not understand what you mean. They believe indeed in the Holy Spirit, but their eyes have not been opened to the fact that more of the Spirit is the one thing needed for the church.

There are others who will agree with you when you speak of this need and yet will really give you even less encouragement.

They have often thought and prayed over the matter, but no benefit has resulted from their effort. They have made no real progress. They urge you to look to the church of earlier times and say that it was not much different than it is now.

These people belong to the generation of the ten spies who were sent to spy out Canaan. The land is glorious, but the enemy in possession is too strong. We are too weak to overcome them. Lack of consecration and of willingness to surrender everything for this blessing is the root of the unbelief and has made them incapable of exercising the courage of Caleb when he said, *"Let us go up at once and take possession, for we are well able to overcome it"* (Num. 13:30).

If you wish to be filled with the Spirit, do not allow yourself to be held back by such reasonings. Only believe and strengthen yourself in the omnipotence of God. Do not say, "Is God able?" Say, rather, "God is able." The God who was able to raise Christ from the dead (Rom. 8:11) is still mighty in the midst of His people and is able to reveal His divine life with power in your heart.

Hear His voice saying to you as to Abraham, *"I am Almighty God; walk before Me and be blameless"* (Gen. 17:1). Set your heart without distraction on what God has said that He will do and then on the omnipotence that is prepared to bring the promise to accomplishment.

Pray to the Father that He will grant you to be strengthened with might by His Spirit (Eph. 3:16). Adore Him who is able to do for us *"exceedingly abundantly above all that we ask and think"* (v. 20), and give Him the glory.

Let faith in the omnipotence of God fill your soul, and you will be full of the assurance that, however difficult, however improbable, however impossible it may seem, God can fill us with His Spirit. *"Only believe"* (Mark 5:36).

HE WILL WORK IT IN YOU

When one prays for this blessing of being filled with the Spirit, the thought will spring up uninvited of what one's life as a Christian has already been. The believer thinks of all the workings of divine grace in his heart and of the incessant striving of the Spirit. He thinks of all his efforts and prayers, of his past attempts at entire surrender, and of the taking hold of faith. He then looks on what he is at the moment, on his unfaithfulness and sin and helplessness, and he becomes dispirited. In the span of many years, little progress has been made. The past testifies only of failure and unfaithfulness.

If all his praying and believing of earlier days have been of so little avail, why should he now dare to hope that everything is to be transformed at once? He presents to himself the life of a man full of the Holy Spirit, and alongside it he sets his own life as he has learned to know it. It becomes impossible for him to imagine that he will ever be able to live as a man full of the Spirit. For such a task he is unfit and feels no courage to make the attempt.

Christian, when such thoughts as these crowd in on you, there is only one bit of advice to follow, and that is, *"Only believe."* Cast yourself into the arms of your Father who gives His children the Holy Spirit much more readily than an earthly father gives bread. Only believe and count on the love of God. All your self-dedication and surrender, all your faith and integrity, are not works by which you have to move God or make Him willing to bless you. Far from it.

God desires to bless you and will Himself work everything in you. God loves you as a Father and sees that, to be able to live in perfect health and happiness as His child, you have need of nothing but this one thing—to be full of His Spirit. Jesus has by His blood opened up the way to the full enjoyment of this love.

Enter into this love, abide in this love, and by faith acknowledge that it shines on and surrounds you, even as the light of the sun illuminates and animates your body. Begin to trust this love. I do not say trust in its willingness, but in its unspeakable longing to fill you entirely with itself. Your Father's love waits to make you full of His Spirit. He Himself will do it for you.

And what does He crave at your hands? Simply this, that you yield yourself to Him in utter unworthiness, nothingness, and powerlessness to let Him do this work in you. Taking charge of all the preparatory work, God will help you by His Spirit. He will strengthen you with might in the inner man, silently and hiddenly, to abandon everything that has to be given up to receive this treasure. He will help you to rest in His Word and to wait for Him in faith. He will hold Himself responsible for all the future. He will make provision that you will be able to walk in the fullness of this blessing.

Perhaps you have already formed a very high idea of what a man must be who is filled with the Spirit of God, and you see no chance of your being able to live in such a fashion. Or it may be that you have not been able to form any idea of it whatsoever and are, on that account, afraid to strive for a life that is so unknown to you. Christian, abandon all such thoughts. The

Spirit alone, once He is in you, will Himself teach you what that life is, for He will work it in you. God will take upon Himself the responsibility of making you full of the Spirit, not as a treasure that you must carry and keep, but as a power that is to carry and keep you. Therefore, *"only believe"* (Mark 5:36). Count on the love of your Father.

n His promise of the blessing and the power of the Spirit, the Lord Jesus always pointed to God the Father. He called it *"the Promise of My Father"* (Luke 24:49). He directed us to the faithfulness of God. *"He who promised is faithful"* (Heb. 10:23). He directed us to the power of God. The Spirit was, as power from on high, to come from God Himself. (See Acts 1:8.) He directed us to the love of God. It is as a Father that God is to give this gift to His children.

Let every thought of this blessing and every desire for it only lead us to God. Here is something that He must do, that He must give, that He, He alone, must work. Let us in silent adoration set our hearts on God. Let us joyfully trust in Him. He is able to do abundantly above all praying and thinking.

His love will willingly bestow a full blessing on us. God will make you full of the Spirit. Say humbly, "Behold the servant of the Lord. Let Him do to me what is good in His sight. Be it unto me according to Your Word." (See Luke 1:38.) *"He who calls you is faithful, who also will do it"* (1 Thess. 5:24).

11

FINDING THE BLESSING

Then I will sprinkle clean water on you, and you shall be clean; I will cleanse you from all your filthiness and from all your idols. I will...put a new spirit within you....I will put My Spirit within you and cause you to walk in My statutes, and you will keep My judgments and do them.
—Ezekiel 36:25–27

The full Pentecostal blessing is for all the children of God. *"As many as are led by the Spirit of God, these are sons of God"* (Rom. 8:14). God does not give a half portion to any one of His children. To every one He says, *"Son, you are always with me, and all that I have is yours"* (Luke 15:31). Christ is not divided (see 1 Corinthians 1:13); he who receives Him receives Him in all His fullness. Every Christian is destined by God and is actually called to be filled with the Spirit.

In the preceding chapters I have had in view especially those who are to some extent acquainted with these things and have been already in search of the truth. They have already been led, after conversion, to make a more complete renunciation of sin and to yield themselves wholly to the Lord. But it is quite conceivable that among those who read this book, there may be Christians who have heard little of the full Pentecostal blessing and in whose hearts the desire has arisen to obtain a share in it. They do not, however, understand that they are willing to have pointed out to them where they are to begin and what they have to do in order to succeed in their desire. They are prepared to acknowledge that their lives are full of sin and that it seems to them as if they will have to strive long and earnestly before they can become full of the Spirit.

I would like to inspire them with fresh courage and to direct them to the God who has said, *"I, the Lord, will hasten it in its time"* (Isa. 60:22). I would like to take them and guide them to the place where God will bless them and to point to them out of His Word what the attitude must be in which they can receive this blessing.

PUTTING AWAY SIN

In the message of Ezekiel, God first promised, *"I will cleanse you,"* and then, *"I will put My Spirit within you."* A vessel into which anything precious is to be poured must always first be cleansed. So, if the Lord is to give you a new and full blessing, a new cleansing must also take place.

Your conversion was a confession and putting away of sin. After conversion you endeavored to overcome sin, but the effort did not succeed because you did not know the purity and holiness the Lord desired.

This new cleansing must come through new confession and discovery of sin. The old leaven cannot be purged unless it is first searched for and found. Do not say that you already know sufficiently well that your Christian life is full of sin. Sit down in silent meditation with the specific purpose of seeing what your life as a Christian has been. How much pride, self-seeking, worldliness, self-will, and impurity has been in it? Can such a heart receive the fullness of the Spirit? It is impossible.

Look into your home life. Do hastiness of temper, anxiety about yourself, bitterness, harsh or unbecoming words testify to how little you have been cleansed?

Look into the current life of the church. How much religion is there that is merely intellectual, formal, and pleasing to men, without real humiliation of spirit? It lacks real desire for the living God, real love for Jesus, and real subjection to the Word—things that constitute worship in spirit and in truth.

Look into your general course of conduct. Consider whether the people around you can testify that they have observed, by your honorable spirit and freedom from worldly-mindedness, that you are one who has been cleansed from sin by God. Contemplate all this in the light of what God expects from you and has offered to work in you, and take your place as a guilty, helpless soul that must be cleansed before God can bestow the full blessing on you.

NOT IN OUR OWN STRENGTH

Following this discovery is the actual putting away and casting out of what is impure. This is something that you are simply bound to do. You must come with these sins, especially with those that are most strictly your own troublesome sins. You must acknowledge them before God in confession and make renunciation of them.

You must be brought to the conviction that your life is a guilty and shameful life. You are not at liberty to take comfort in the consideration that you are so weak or that the majority of Christians live no higher life than you. It must become a matter of earnest resolution with you that your life is to undergo a complete transformation. The sins that still cleave to you are to be cast off and done away with.

Perhaps you may say in reply that you find yourself unable to do away with them or cast them off. I tell you that you are quite able to do this. You can give these sins up to God. If there happens to be anything in my house that I wish to have taken away and I am unable to carry, I call for men who will do it for me. I give it over into their hands, saying, "Look here, take that away," and they do it. So I am able to say that I have put the thing out of my house.

In like manner, you can give up to God those sins of yours against which you feel yourself utterly powerless. You can give them up to Him to be dealt with as He desires, and He will fulfill His promise: *"I will cleanse you from all your filthiness."*

There should be a definite understanding between you and the Lord. You on your part must confess your sin and bid it everlasting farewell. Wait on Him until He assures you that He has taken your heart and life into His own hands to give you complete victory.

EXPERIENCING CHRIST

If the knowledge of sin at conversion is superficial, so also is the faith in Jesus. Our faith, our reception of Jesus, never goes further or deeper than our insight into sin. If since your conversion you have learned to know the inward, invincible power of sin in your life, you are now prepared to receive from God a discovery of the inward, invincible power of the Lord Jesus in your heart as you have never known it before.

If you really long for a complete deliverance from sin, to be able to live in obedience to God, God will reveal the Lord Jesus to you as a complete Savior. He will make you know that although the flesh, with its inclination to evil, always remains in you, the Lord Jesus will so dwell in your heart so that the power of the flesh will be kept in subjection by Him. Then you will no longer do the will of the flesh.

Through Jesus Christ, God will cleanse you from all unrighteousness so that, day by day, you may walk before God with a pure heart. What you really need is the discovery that He is prepared to work this change in you. You may receive it by faith here and now.

This is what Jesus Christ desires to work in you by the Holy Spirit. He came to put away sin—not the guilt and punishment of it only, but sin itself. He has not only mastered the power and dominion of the law and its curse over you, but He has also completely broken and taken away the power and dominion of sin. He has completely rescued you as a newborn soul from beneath the power of sin. He lives in His heavenly authority and all-pervading presence in order to work out this deliverance in you.

In this power, He will live in you and carry out His work in you. As the indwelling Christ, He is bent on maintaining and manifesting His redemption in you. The sins that you have confessed—the pride, the lovelessness, the worldly-mindedness, and uncleanness—He will by His power take out of your heart.

Although the flesh may tempt you, the choice and the joy of your heart must abide in Him and in His obedience to God's will. Yes, you may indeed become more than a conqueror through Him who loves you. (See Romans 8:37.) As the indwelling Christ, He will overcome sin in you.

What, then, is required on our side? When the soul sees it to be true that Jesus will carry out this work, it will then open the door before Him and receive Him into the heart as Lord and King. Yes, this can be done at once. A house that has remained closely shut for twenty years can be penetrated by the light in a moment if the doors and windows are thrown open. In like manner, a heart that has remained enveloped in darkness and powerlessness for twenty years, because it did not know that Jesus was willing to take the victory over sin into His own hands, can have its whole experience changed in a moment.

When I acknowledge my sinful condition, yield myself to God, and trust the Lord to do this work, then I may firmly believe that it is done and that Jesus takes all that is in me into His own hands. This is an act of faith that must be held fast. When doors and windows are thrown open and the light streaming in drives out the darkness, we discover at once how much dust and impurity there is in the house. But the light shines in order that we may see how to take it away.

When we receive Christ into the heart, everything is not yet perfected. Light and gladness are not seen and experienced at once, but by faith the soul knows that He who is faithful will keep His Word and will surely do His work. The faith that has, up to this moment, only sought and wrestled, now rests in the Lord and His Word.

It knows that what was begun by faith must be carried forward only by faith. It says, "I abide in Jesus; I know that He abides in me and that He will manifest Himself to me." As Jesus cleansed the lepers with a word, so He cleanses us by His Word. He who firmly holds to this fact in faith will see the proof of it.

PREPARING YOUR SOUL

The Lord gave the promise, "I will cleanse you." Then He gave the second promise, "I will put My Spirit within you." The Holy Spirit cannot come with power or fill the heart and continue to dwell in it, unless a special and complete cleansing first takes place within it.

The Spirit and sin are engaged in mortal combat. The only reason why the Spirit works so feebly in the church is sin, which is all too little known or dreaded or cast out. Men do not believe in the power of Christ to cleanse; therefore, He cannot do His work of baptizing with the Spirit.

It is from Christ that the Spirit comes and to Christ the Spirit returns again. The heart that gives Christ liberty to exercise dominion in it will inherit the full blessing.

Reader, if you have done what has been suggested, if you have believed in Jesus as the Lord who cleanses you, be assured that God will certainly fulfill His Word: *"I will cleanse you… [and] put My Spirit within you."* Cling to Jesus, who cleanses you. Let Him be all within you. God will see to it that you are filled with the Spirit.

Do not be surprised if your heart does not at once feel as you would like it to feel immediately after your act of surrender. Rest assured that if you present yourself to God as a pure vessel, cleansed by Christ, to be filled with the Spirit, God will take you at your word and say to you, *"Receive the Holy Spirit"* (John 20:22). He will manifest it to you more gloriously than ever before.

Keep in mind the purpose for which the Spirit is given. God said He would put His Spirit within you and cause you to walk in His statutes and keep His judgments and do them. The fullness of the Spirit must be sought and received with the direct aim that you will now simply and wholly live to do God's will and work on the earth. Yes, you will be able to live like the Lord Jesus and to say with Him, *"Behold, I have come…to do Your will, O God"* (Heb. 10:7).

If you cherish this disposition, the fullness of the Spirit may be positively expected. Be full of courage and yield yourself to walk in God's statutes and to keep His judgments and do them, and you may trust God to keep His Word that He will cause you to keep and do them. He, the living God, will work in you. Even before you are aware how the Spirit is in you, He will enable you to experience the full blessing.

Have you been seeking for a long while without finding the fullness of the Spirit? Here you have at last the sure method of winning it. Acknowledge the sinfulness of your condition as a Christian, and make renunciation of it once and for all by yielding it up to God. Acknowledge that the Lord Jesus is ready and able to cleanse your heart from its sin, to conquer these sins by His entrance into it, and to set you free.

Take Him now as your Lord, at once and forever. Be assured that He will do it. Permit Him to begin, and let Him do it in you now.

12

THE KEY TO THE SECRET

*Then the Son Himself will also be subject to Him who put
all things under Him, that God may be all in all.*
—1 Corinthians 15:28

When we speak of entire consecration, we are frequently
asked what the precise distinction is between the ordinary doctrine of sanctification and the preaching of the gracious work
that has begun to prevail in the church in recent years. One
answer that may be given is that the distinction lies solely in the
little word "all." This word is the key to the secret. The ordinary

method of proclaiming the necessity of holiness is true as far as it goes, but sufficient emphasis is not laid on this one point of the "*all.*"

Why, then, is the fullness of the Spirit not more widely enjoyed? That little word "*all*" suggests the explanation. As long as the "*all*" of God, of sin, of Christ, of surrender, of the Spirit, and of faith is not fully understood, the soul cannot enjoy all that God wants it to be.

Let us consider the full Pentecostal blessing from this standpoint. Do this in a spirit of humble waiting on God and with the prayer that He will make us, by His Spirit, feel where the evil lies and what the remedy is. Then we will be ready to give up everything in order to receive nothing less than everything.

THE ALL OF GOD

The answer lies in the very being and nature of God that He must be all. "*Of Him and through Him and to Him are all things*" (Rom. 11:36). As God, He is the life of everything. Everything that exists serves as a means for the manifestation of the goodness, wisdom, and power of God in His direct and continuous operation.

Sin consists in nothing but the fact that man determined to be something and would not allow God to be everything. The redemption of Jesus has no other aim than that God should again become everything in our hearts and lives. In the end, even the Son will be subjected to the Father so that God may be all in all. Nothing less than this is what redemption is to secure. Christ Himself has shown in His life what it means to be nothing and to allow God to be everything. As He once lived on the earth, so does He still live in the hearts of His people. According to the measure in which they receive the truth that God is all, the fullness of the blessing will be able to find its way into their lives.

The all of God—this is what we must seek. In His will, His honor, and His power, He must be everything for us. There should be no word of our lips, no movement of our hearts, no satisfying of the needs of our physical lives, that is not the expression of the will, glory, and power of God. Only the man who discerns this and consents to it can rightly understand what the fullness of the Spirit must bring about and why it is necessary for us to forsake everything if we desire to obtain it. God must be not merely something, not merely much, but literally all.

THE ALL OF SIN

What is sin? It is separation from God. Where man is guided by his own will, his own honor, or his own power; where the will, the honor, and the operation of God are not manifested, sin must be at work. Sin is death and misery because it is a turning away from God to the creature.

Sin is in no sense a thing that may exist in man along with other things that are good. No, as God was once everything, so has sin in fallen man become everything. It now dominates and penetrates his whole being, even as God should have been allowed to do. Every part of his nature is corrupt. We still have our natural existence in God. All is in sin and under the influence of sin.

The all of sin—some small measure of the knowledge of this fact was necessary even at the time of conversion. This, however, was still very imperfect. If a Christian is to make progress and become fully convinced of the necessity of being filled with the Spirit, his eyes must be opened to the extent in which sin dominates everything within him.

Everything in him is tainted with sin, and therefore the omnipotence of God must take in hand the renewal of everything by the Holy Spirit. Man is utterly powerless to do what is good in the highest sense. He can do no more of what is good than what the Spirit actually works in him at any moment. He learns also to see the all of sin just as distinctly in the world around him. Everything must be sacrificed and given over to death.

All of God must expel the all of sin. God must again live wholly and entirely within us and continually take the place that sin usurped. He who desires this change will rightly understand and desire the fullness of the Spirit, and as he believes he will certainly receive it.

THE ALL OF CHRIST

The Son is the revelation of the Father—the all of God is exhibited to our view and made accessible to us in the Son. On this account, the all of Christ is just as necessary and infinite as that of God. Christ is God come upon the earth to undo the all of sin, to win back and restore in man the lost all of God. To this end we must thoroughly know the all of Christ.

The idea that most believing disciples have of the all of Christ is that He alone does everything in the atonement and the forgiveness of sin. This is indeed the glorious beginning of His redemptive work, but still only the beginning. God has given in Him all that we have need of life and grace. Christ Himself desires to be our life and strength, the Indweller of our hearts, who animates our hearts and makes them what they ought to be before God. To know the all of Christ and to understand how Christ is prepared to be everything in us is the secret of true sanctification. He who discerns the will of God in this principle and yields himself to its operation has found the pathway to the full blessing of Pentecost.

Acknowledge the all of Christ in humble, joyful thanksgiving. Confess that everything has been given by God in Him. Receive with firm confidence the fact that Christ is all and the promise that He will work all, yes, all in you. Consent from the heart that this must be so, and confirm it by laying everything at His feet and offering it up to Him. The two things go together: let Him be and do all, and let Him reign and rule over all. Let there be nothing in which He does not rule and operate. It is not impossible for you to accomplish this change. Let Him be everything; let Him have everything in order that by His almighty energy He may fill everything with Himself.

THE ALL OF SURRENDER

Leave all, sell all, forsake all—this was the Lord's requirement when He was here on earth. The requirement is still in force. The chief hindrance of the Christian life is that, because men do not believe that Christ is all, they consequently never think of the necessity of giving Him all.

Everything must be given to Him, because everything is under sin. He cannot cleanse and keep a thing when it is not yielded up to Him so that He can take full possession of it and fill it. All must be given up to Him, because He alone can bring the all of God to its rightful supremacy within us. Even what appears useful or lawful or innocent becomes defiled by the stain of our selfishness when it is held fast in our own possession and for our own enjoyment. We must surrender it into the hands and the power of Christ; only there can it be sanctified.

The all of surrender—it is because Christians are so ignorant of this requirement that all their praying and hearing avail so little. If you are really prepared to turn to God for the fullness of the Spirit and to have your heart purified and kept pure, then be assured that it is your blessed privilege to regard and deal with everything—everything that you have to strive for or do—as given up to Him. The all of surrender will be the measure of your experience of the all of Christ.

In a preceding chapter we have seen that surrender may be carried out at once and as a whole. Let us not merely think of this, but actually do it. Yes, this very day, let the all of Christ be the power of a surrender on our part that will be immediate, complete, and everlasting.

THE ALL OF THE SPIRIT

The all of God and the all of Christ demand as a necessary consequence the all of the Spirit. It is the work of the Spirit to glorify the Son as dwelling in us and by Him to reveal the Father. How can He do this if He Himself is not all and does not penetrate all with His own power? To be filled with the Spirit, to let the Spirit have all, is indispensable to a true, healthy Christian life.

It is a source of great loss in the life of Christendom today that the truth is not discerned that the triune God must have all. Even the professing Christian often makes it his very first aim to find out what he is and what he desires, what pleases him and makes him happy. Then he brings in God in the second place to secure this happiness. The claim of God is not the primary or main consideration. He does not discern that God must have him at His disposal even in the most trivial details of his life in order to manifest His divine glory in him. He is not aware that this entire filling with the will and the operation of God would prove to be his highest happiness. He does not know that the very same Christ, who once lived on the earth entirely surrendered to the will of the Father, is prepared to abide and work in like manner in his heart and life now. It is on this account that he can never fully comprehend how necessary it is that the Spirit must be all and must fill him completely.

If these thoughts have had any influence with you, allow yourself to be brought to the acknowledgment that the Spirit must be all in you. Say from the heart, "I am not at liberty to make any, even the least, exception—the Spirit must have all." Then add to this confession the simple thought that Christ has come to restore the all of God, and the Spirit has been given to reveal the all of Christ within us. Remember that the love of the Father is eagerly longing to secure again His own supreme place with us. Then your heart will be filled with the sure confidence that the Father actually gives you the fullness of the Spirit.

THE ALL OF FAITH

"All things are possible to him who believes" (Mark 9:23). *"Whatever things you ask when you pray, believe that you receive*

them, and you will have them" (Mark 11:24). The preceding sections of this chapter have taught us to understand why it is that faith is all. It is because God is all. It is because man is nothing and has nothing good in him except the capacity for receiving God. When he becomes a believer, what God reveals becomes of itself a heavenly light that illuminates him. He sees then what God is prepared to be for him, and he keeps his soul silent before God and open to God. He gives God the opportunity to work all by the Spirit. The more unceasingly and undividedly he believes, the more fully the all of God and Christ can prevail and work in him.

The all of faith—how little it is understood in the church that the one and only thing I have to do is to keep my soul open before God so that He may be free to work in me. This faith, as the willing acceptance and expectation of God's working, receives all and can achieve all. Every glance at my own powerlessness or sin, every glance at the promise of God and His power to fulfill it, must rouse me to the gladness of faith that God is able to work all.

Let such a faith look on Christ today and move you to renounce every known sin and receive Him as One who purifies you. Oh, that faith might receive the all of Christ and take Him with all that He is! Oh, that your faith might see that the all of the Spirit is your rightful heritage and that your hope is sure that the full blessing has been bestowed on you by God Himself!

If the all of God, the all of Christ, and the all of the Spirit are so immeasurable, if the dominion and power of the terrible all of sin is so unlimited, if the all of your surrender to God and your decision to live wholly for Him is so real, then let your faith in what God will do for you also be unlimited. *"He who believes in Me,…out of his heart will flow rivers of living water"* (John 7:38).

Reader, there is something that can be done today. The Holy Spirit says, *"Today, if you will hear His voice: do not harden your hearts"* (Ps. 95:7–8). I cannot promise that you will immediately overflow with the light and joy of the Holy Spirit. I do not promise you that you will today feel very holy and truly blessed. But what can take place is this: today you may receive Christ as One who purifies, baptizes, and fills you with the Spirit.

Yes, today you may surrender your whole being to Him to be forever wholly under the mastery of the Spirit. Today you may acknowledge and take hold of the all of the Spirit as your personal possession. Today you may submit to the requirement of the all of faith and begin to live only and wholly in the faith of what Christ will do in you through the Spirit.

This you may do; this you ought to do. Kneel down at the mercy seat and do it. Read once more the earlier chapter that deals with what Christ is prepared to do, and surrender yourself this very hour as an empty vessel to be filled with the Spirit. In His own time, God will certainly accomplish it in you.

There is also something, however, that He on His part is prepared to do. Today He is ready to give you the assurance that He accepts your surrender and to seal on your heart the conviction that the fullness of the Spirit belongs to you. Wait on Him to give you this today!

Pay close attention to my last words. The all of God summons you. The all of sin summons you. The all of Christ summons you. The all of the surrender that Jesus requires summons you. The all of the Spirit, His indispensableness and His glory, summons you. The all of faith summons you. Come and let the love of God conquer you. Come and let the glorious salvation master you. Do not back away from the glorious tidings that the triune God is prepared to be your all. Be silent and listen to it until your soul becomes constrained to give the answer, "Even in me God will be all." Take Christ anew today as One who has given His life so that God may be all. Yield your life for this supreme end. God will fill you also with His Holy Spirit.